CHE GUEVARA

A Life

CHE GUEVARA
A Life

Nick Caistor

Interlink Books

An imprint of Interlink Publishing Group, Inc.
Northampton, Massachusetts

First published in 2010 by

INTERLINK BOOKS
An imprint of Interlink Puiiblishing Group, Inc.
46 Crosby Street, Northampton, Massachusetts 01060
www.interlinkbooks.com

Library of Congress Cataloging-in-Publication Data
Caistor, Nick.
Che Guevara : a life / by Nick Caistor.
    p. cm.
Includes bibliographical references and index.
ISBN 978-1-56656-759-6 (pbk.)
1. Guevara, Ernesto, 1928–1967. 2. Guerrillas—Latin America—Biography.
3. Cuba—History—1959–1990. 4. Latin America—History—1948–1980. I. Title.
F2849.22.G85C281114 2009
980.03'5092—dc22   [B]
                                    2009028800

The author and publishers would like to thank the following for permission to reproduce
their photographs: **akg-images**/ullstein bild p75; **Camera Press**/5356/Gamma p51, p64,
Camera Press/OAH/Jazz Editions/Gamma p13, p16, Camera Press/PR/LAT p5, p6;
Getty Images/AFP p102, p111; **Mary Evans Picture Library**/Rue Des Archives p27(t);
PA Photos/Andrew St George p59, PA Photos/AP p85, p93, PA Photos/DPA/Deutsche
Press Agentur/DP, PA Photos/Esteban Felix/AP p139, PA Photos/Joe Cavaretta/AP
p129; **Topfoto**/AP p119, p127

Book design by Juliana Spear

Cover image of Guevara © AP Images
Cover image of Havana © Basilisk/Dreamstime.com

Printed and bound in the United States of America

To request our 48-page full-color catalog, please visit our website at:
www.interlinkbooks.com, call us toll-free at: 1-800-238-LINK, or write to us at:
Interlink Publishing, 46 Crosby Street, Northampton, MA 01060

CONTENTS

INTRODUCTION:
THE LAST ARMED PROPHET

O ne of the most instantly recognizable and influential
figures in twentieth-century Caribbean history, Ernesto
"Che" Guevara began his life several thousand miles
from the region. If he played a hugely important role in
changing the course of Cuba's history in the second half of the
twentieth century, he lived on the island for less than a decade,
and was a Cuban citizen for fewer than seven years. Yet though
born in distant Argentina in 1928, there is no doubt that Cuba
and the Caribbean gave Guevara the chance to apply his ideals
and convictions directly in the real world. Although by
temperament he was a perpetual outsider, the political and
social injustices he found in 1950s Cuba helped him focus his
seemingly limitless energies on a single project: to bring about
revolutionary change in order to transform society and each
and every individual living in it.

Che Guevara was also fortunate in meeting the man who
proved to be the perfect foil for his own qualities of devotion to
a cause: the Cuban revolutionary Fidel Castro. Much has been
written about their hugely different personalities and
approaches to politics and to life. It has often been said that,
after the success of their revolutionary campaign and the
installation of a new regime in Cuba, the two men could not
agree on the path to take.

Some writers have even suggested that Fidel sent Guevara
on his final, fatal expedition to Bolivia in order to be rid of him
once and for all. What seems more likely is that the bonds of
mutual respect forged during the long months of precarious
struggle in the Sierra Maestra mountains of Cuba from 1956 to
1958 were stronger than any political divergences. If Che went
to Bolivia and almost certain failure in 1966, it had much more
to do with the forces driving him ever since he left his native

Argentina in 1951 on his first voyage of discovery: a need to expose himself to the often harsh realities of the continent, and to play as prominent a role as possible in changing those realities according to principles he also discovered as he went along.

It is sometimes hard to judge exactly what Che Guevara's personal qualities were from the accounts of those who knew him or have written about him. According to the official Cuban version, promoted by everyone from Fidel Castro downwards, Che was the model revolutionary, the man who sacrificed himself entirely for the cause, without thought for his own comfort, ambition or personal safety. He was the model of the revolutionary "new man," the kind of person he himself wrote about in his essay on *Man and Socialism in Cuba* in 1965. Here he described how individuals could fully realize their potential only when they had absorbed the lessons of socialism and its basic tenet: "from each according to their ability, to each according to their need." For many years after his death in 1967, Cuban schoolchildren used to start their day with the slogan: "We will all be like Che," while government officials and party activists would chant: *sus enseñanzas fortalecen nuestro trabajo* ("his teachings strengthen our work"). In 2006 Fidel Castro delivered this verdict on him:

> Che symbolized the highest human values, and he was an extraordinary example. He created a great aura, a great mystique. I admired him a great deal, and loved him. It always produces a great deal of affection, that admiration.

Those at the opposite end of the political spectrum to Guevara and Castro do not share that affection. The right-wing view of him was put most trenchantly in the international business magazine *The Economist* on the occasion of the fortieth anniversary of his death in October 2007:

> Rather than a Christian romantic, Guevara was a ruthless and dogmatic Marxist, who stood not for liberation but for a new tyranny. In the Sierra Maestra, he shot those suspected of treachery; in victory, Mr. Castro placed him in charge of

the firing squads that executed "counter-revolutionaries"; as minister of industries, Guevara advocated expropriation down to the last farm and shop. His exhortation to guerrilla warfare, irrespective of political circumstance, lured thousands of idealistic Latin Americans to their deaths, helped to create brutal dictatorships and delayed the achievement of democracy.

Che Guevara was only thirty-nine when he met a miserable end in the wilds of Bolivia. This early death made it easy for him to become the model of the "heroic *guerrillero*" which has not merely lasted but has grown even stronger over the years since he was killed. In Cuba, he very soon became part of the pantheon of national heroes, alongside José Martí and Camilo Cienfuegos. It is striking that it is Che's image rather than that of Fidel which dominates the central public square in Havana, where a five-storey high portrait of him hangs on the side of the Ministry of the Interior building overlooking Revolution Square. He also provided the Cuban state media with a perfect opportunity for glorification; the ICAIC (Cuban Institute for Cinematographic Art and Industry) made propaganda films of his participation in the revolutionary struggle, and the state-run recording industry produced a wide variety of popular songs about "Comandante Che Guevara" and the example he set.

It was not only in Cuba that Che Guevara quickly became a symbol of revolutionary endeavor and purity. Throughout Latin America, and in particular in his native Argentina, his figure was a rallying point for the radical movements espoused by a new generation. Many young people were convinced by his idea of the revolutionary *foco*—the attack on established regimes by a small, totally committed group who would quickly win converts and expose the basically oppressive nature of "bourgeois" rule, sweeping away the rotten governments and replacing them with truly democratic rule by "the people." All too often, this was seen as a shortcut that could do away with the need to build any real mass movement based on class or identity of interest, rebellions in which violence took the place of argument and persuasion.

This view of Che as the revolutionary hero who was the model of a way of life and action was also taken up by dissident youth in the United States and Europe. This generation was anxious to shake the old order which it saw as standing in the way of freedom and equality. For many, Che Guevara's life seemed to prove that the world could be changed sooner rather than later, and that individual will rather than adherence to any "scientific" doctrine was the most valuable quality that could help usher in such change. Despite the violent disruptions of 1968 in the United States and Europe, often inspired by this idea of Che's legacy, the hope that western capitalist society could be easily overthrown was soon thwarted. The more extreme left-wing groups were quickly snuffed out in the developed capitalist world, while in Latin America attempts to bring in socialism or to achieve "national liberation" from US imperialism were crushed by some of the most brutal military dictatorships ever seen on the continent. Only in Nicaragua in 1979 did some of the seeds of Guevara's promotion of revolutionary movements appear to bear fruit, when the rebel Sandinistas ousted the dynastic Somoza family and tried to put into practice their socialist beliefs. As Che Guevara himself had predicted almost two decades earlier, however, Washington could not allow the revolution to thrive, and used every means possible short of direct military intervention to bring about the downfall of the revolutionary regime, which surrendered power at the ballot box in 1989.

This was also the year when the collapse of the communist regimes in Eastern Europe became dramatically evident. Marxist theory crumbled under the weight of reality, as citizens chose the capitalist market and freedom as consumers over the threadbare promises of communism. What had been a "bipolar world," as the Cubans called it, was now "unipolar," with globalized capitalism and the United States' model as apparently the only available option.

In this globalized world, the image of Che Guevara survived, and fulfilled two very different functions. On the one hand, he was promoted as an icon to sell everything from ice-cream (Cherry Guevara flavor) to dark glasses, from the ubiquitous T-shirt to tattoos on the arms of the internationally famous (from the heavyweight boxer and "bad boy" Mike Tyson to the Argentine footballer Diego Maradona). Che Guevara as a brand name was cleverly exploited as a symbol of the "rebel" consumer—the canny individual who can see through the game of the big companies, and is able to assert his or her own distinctive individuality. On the other, his name and image have been used to represent a challenge to authority in any guise, a "cry for freedom" that no longer has any specific meaning to it. In this short biography, my aim is to provide readers with enough information about Che Guevara's life and writings to be able to make up their own minds about his value to them today. He was a man in a hurry to learn about the world, and to put what he had learned to the test. More than forty years after his death, Che Guevara continues to fascinate and intrigue people all over the world. This book tries to bring to the fore the man and the context in which he lived and fought, to provide information for a better appreciation of him than one based solely on an image on a wall or t-shirt.

1
ARGENTINA AND BEYOND
(1928–1953)

Ernesto Guevara de la Serna was born in Rosario, Argentina's third city on the banks of the River Paraná, on June 14, 1928.

That the future guerrilla and revolutionary was born here was something of an accident, as his father and mother were living much further north at the time, on a plantation where his father Ernesto Guevara Lynch had taken his bride soon after their wedding at the end of 1927, and where he was hoping to make his fortune. When his wife Celia Guevara de la Serna became pregnant and the birth of their first child grew imminent, the young couple decided it would be safer to have the child in the capital city of Buenos Aires, where the medical attention was better and they would be surrounded by family and friends. They had only reached as far as Rosario, however, when Celia went into labor.

Ernesto Guevara was born at around three in the afternoon at the city's Hospital Centenario[1]. The family stayed only a few days in Rosario, and nowadays there is little to mark the arrival of this historic figure, apart from a small plaque in the nearby Plaza de la Co-operación which hails "a son of Rosario who fought for a world with more justice and solidarity."

At the end of the 1920s, the city of Rosario was a typical example of how Argentina was booming as an agricultural power, with a huge influx of immigrants drawn to it in the hope of escaping poverty and growing political chaos in Europe. Argentina itself still enjoyed democratic rule, with the Radical Civic Union under Hipólito Yrigoyen in power, although the traditional politics dominated by the Radical and Conservative parties was soon interrupted when in 1930 the first of many military coups undermined Argentina's political life.

Apart from the politics, the Argentina that Ernesto was born into was in the throes of profound change. In part, this was due to massive and rapid shifts in population. When his parents were born in the late 1890s, Argentina was a country of around four million people, its economy still rooted in agriculture and exports of beef and wheat. By the late 1920s, Argentina's cities, like Buenos Aires, Córdoba and Rosario, were expanding at a spectacular rate, and the balance of population was swiftly changing from mostly rural to urban.

These new Argentines came from many European countries. Unlike Cuba, where Ernesto was later to gain international fame, Argentina had become independent of Spain at the start of the nineteenth century rather than at the end of it. This

---

1 In his major biography on Che in English, Jon Lee Anderson claims that he was, in fact, born a month earlier, on 14 May, but the later date was adopted in an attempt to disguise the fact that Celia had been pregnant when she married Ernesto Guevara Lynch. Whatever the truth, it is interesting to note that, like that of Fidel Castro and other "mythical" heroes, Che's exact birth date has become a source of debate and mystery.

meant that from the mid-century onwards, the population was not so much of Spanish stock, but was drawn from very different parts of Europe: Jews who fled pogroms in Russia and the Ukraine, agricultural laborers from Italy, migrants from Britain and Ireland who came to build the railways, port facilities and services, and then stayed on to run them.

The family of Ernesto's father, Ernesto Guevara Lynch, had Irish roots as well as Spanish. In the 1840s his father had left Argentina to join the gold rush in California, demonstrating a sense of adventure apparently shared by all the Guevara males. On his mother's side, the links with Spain were even stronger; one ancestor had been the viceroy of Peru in colonial times, another a famous general. Celia de la Serna's father had been an ambassador and congressman, and although he died when she was still a young girl, she brought considerable wealth to her marriage through her inheritance.

The burgeoning population and thriving cities meant that many people in Argentina sought to make fortunes from new openings. Ernesto's father was one of these; he was constantly looking (usually unsuccessfully) for the business opportunity that would make his fortune and cement the family's position in Argentina's upper middle class. When his son Ernesto—the first of five children—was born, Guevara Lynch was trying to make money from a *yerba mate* tea plantation in Misiones, a province in the far north of Argentina close to the border with Brazil and Paraguay. The bitter herb drink was enjoying new-found popularity among middle-class Argentines, and Guevara Lynch was hoping to cash in on the fashion (using his wife's inheritance to buy the land).

A few weeks after the "accidental" birth in Rosario, the tiny Ernestito as he was known (the nickname "Che" only came much later, during the guerrilla struggle in Cuba, where all Argentines are known affectionately as *che*, as this is a word Argentines uniquely add as a tag to the end of sentences—its original meaning is apparently from one of the country's indigenous languages, where it means "man") was taken back to the plantation in the hot jungle region of north-east Argentina. It was not many months before one of the defining characteristics of his life began to make an appearance. One day, after Ernesto had been swimming in a river with his mother, he had a violent coughing fit. The doctors at first diagnosed the incident as bronchitis, but when it persisted, decided that the youngster had severe asthma. This illness and his strenuous attempts to overcome it and lead as active a life as possible were to mark Che forever. It may well have been the reason for his early choice of medicine as a career, but before that, it caused his family a great deal of heartache. Many years later, his father spoke of the illness in rather uncharitable terms:

> Ernesto's asthma had begun to affect our decisions. Each day there were new restrictions on our freedom of movement, and each day we found ourselves increasingly at the mercy of that infernal illness.

He also recalled how he would spend nights with the young boy on his lap pressed against his chest, as this seemed to be the only position when Ernestito could get some sleep.

From this very early age, the asthma attacks were controlled by injections. But then as now, there was no cure for the illness, and the boy's breathing was quickly affected by the climate, the heat and humidity. The province of Misiones, largely covered in jungle and subject to extreme weather conditions, was probably the worst possible place for the suffering child to be, while the distance from any adequate medical attention was a further worry to his mother. As a result, in 1932 the Guevara family moved to the more clement surroundings of the hills outside the city of Córdoba, a region some three hundred and fifty miles north of the capital Buenos Aires. It is known in the country's history for the foundation of Argentina's first university (by the Jesuits in 1621), and in the 1930s for its sanatoriums and health spas. It was in the small hill resort of Alta Gracia at the foot of the Sierra Chica mountain range that the young Ernesto was to spend the next eleven years.

An early picture of "Che" Guevara as a young boy

"Ernestito" on his father's lap, surrounded by the rest of the family

At first, Ernesto's mother Celia seems to have been very protective of him because of his illness. He did not attend school, but was tutored at home until he was almost nine. She and Guevara Lynch tried to cure his asthma in many ways, from strict diet to making him exercise frequently, but only the dry, gentler climate seems to have had much impact on the attacks, which left him racked with coughing fits or gasping for breath. Many of his biographers have speculated that Guevara's legendary strength of will—and his essentially lonely nature— were forged by the many hours he spent on his own suffering from this chronic illness. His poor health as a young boy undoubtedly also brought him closer to his mother, who seems to have been the stable personality around whom the family gravitated. Ernesto continued to write her candid and heartfelt letters right up until her death in 1965.

Celia de la Serna had been brought up and educated as a Catholic, but unlike most of Cuban guerrilla leaders he was to meet (the Castro brothers and many of the revolutionary high command were educated at Jesuit colleges in Cuba), when Ernesto did go to school it was to the local primary and secondary colleges, which, as with all Argentine state educational establishments, were staunchly nonreligious. The Argentine school system, particularly in urban areas, was generally acknowledged to be among the best on the continent, and Argentina enjoyed the highest rates of literacy and school attendance in Latin America.

At school, Ernesto seems to have been a bright, if not outstanding, student. Many who knew him remarked on his extraordinary passion for reading, and the fact that he began a "philosophical dictionary"—notes on the more serious books he had read—at the age of sixteen. Perhaps unsurprisingly, what most commentators have also noted are the rebellious and leadership qualities the young Guevara was said to have shown. There are many accounts of his daredevilry, whether when playing the upper-class Argentine sport of rugby, or at the head of his own gang of young tearaways in the sedate spa town. These characteristics displayed by the teenage Guevara have led writers such as Jon Lee Anderson to conclude: "his physical fearlessnesss, inclination to lead others, stubbornness, competitive spirit, and self-discipline—all were clearly manifest in the young 'Guevarita' of Alta Gracia."

In 2001 the house on Avellaneda Street in Alta Gracia, where the young Che lived for several years, was opened as a museum. It now attracts thousands of visitors every year; two of the best-known to visit in 2007 were Fidel Castro of Cuba and President Hugo Chávez of Venezuela, who came to pay homage.

The year 1943 saw the Guevara family move into the city of Córdoba, in order to help Ernesto and his brothers and sisters —Celia, Roberto, Juan Martín and Ana María—with their schooling, and in an attempt for their father to secure more regular employment. By this time, the political situation in Argentina had begun to enter a more turbulent phase. Since 1930 the country had been governed either by the military or by a succession of fraudulently elected civilian governments which did their bidding, promoting the traditional interests of Argentina's landowners and "oligarchy"—the small, conservative political power groups that refused to include the new working classes of the big cities, or the indigenous and other poor people in the countryside in the political arena in any meaningful way.

The Second World War put the Argentine political system under fresh strain. President Ortiz, in power since 1937, supported the Allies against the Germans and Italians, both of whom had large expatriate and migrant communities in Argentina. At the start of the war, he banned the Argentine National-Socialist party. It was Ortiz who set up the Acción Argentina committees, of which Ernesto's father was a proud member in Córdoba. These committees were meant to rally support for the Allies and to keep an eye on any suspicious "pro-Nazi" activities. Guevara Lynch enthusiastically joined in such efforts, vigorously denouncing plots and German spies in a region settled by many innocent Germans. The adolescent Ernesto also apparently spied on hotels and other meeting places suspected of harboring Nazi "cells," but this all seems to have been at a very innocent level, without any real political awareness on his part. At the same time, there is no doubt that there were many with genuine fascist leanings in Córdoba, and in 1943 an uprising by the School of Aviation in the city was discovered and quashed at the last minute. (It was also to Córdoba that the head of Hitler's Luftwaffe was brought in 1946 to help build a modern air force for Argentina, and in the late 1970s the School of Aviation there became sadly notorious once more as one of the chief torture centers of the military regime then in power.)

Although the Córboda revolt was foiled, it was in that same year of 1943 that the military stepped in again to take over government. The most powerful group among them was a number of young colonels, including Juan Domingo Perón. What distinguished him from his colleagues was the fact that he saw the political possibilities of giving a prominent role to all those who were traditionally left out of the system. He did this by organizing loyal trade unions and appealing directly to the first- and second-generation immigrants, as well as the rural poor and urban working classes. In so doing, he created the Peronist movement which has dominated Argentina's political life, for good and ill, ever since.

None of the Guevara family showed much enthusiasm for Perón and his movement. For Guevara Lynch, the ideas Perón took from Mussolini's fascism made him suspect. Celia's landowning family was precisely the kind of "oligarchy" the Peronists saw as a target for their political anger, while the teenage Ernesto does not seem to have mixed with the "descamisados"—the poor (hence "shirtless") manual workers who were the mainstay of support for the new political leader in Argentina. It was only when Perón was overthrown in September 1955 that Ernesto, by now a convinced "anti-imperialist," wrote to his Aunt Beatriz from Mexico in the following terms:

> I felt slightly sorry over the fall of Perón. Argentina was a pale gray sheep, but at least it was a bit different from the rest of the flock. Now it will be the same color as its twenty beautiful sisters: the thankful faithful will attend Mass, "respectable" people will be able to put the rabble in its place, the North Americans will invest great amounts of profitable capital in the country, it will be a paradise. I'm not quite sure why, but I miss that little gray-colored sheep.

Later, after the triumph of the revolution in Cuba, Che Guevara went further and forged closer links to the Peronists. He became friendly with John William Cooke, who was the exiled Perón's representative in Havana, and apparently was persuaded that Peronism could become the vanguard of a revolutionary movement in his native country. He also adopted Perón's attempts to counter the "imperialist" media organizations' monopoly of news in the world by setting up the Prensa Latina news agency in Havana, run by the Argentine Jorge Ricardo Masetti (see Chapter Five). Che's lack of identification with Peronism did not, however, prevent a new generation of left-wing guerrillas in Argentina from invoking his name in the late 1960s and early 1970s, when they fought the police and armed forces in an attempt to bring about a "Guevarist" revolution there.

In general, while some biographers of Che have sought to discover a precocious political involvement in Argentine politics that led naturally to his later activities in Cuba, there is little evidence to support the idea. With the defeat of the Spanish Republic in the late 1930s, his father did welcome Spanish exiles into his Córdoba home, and Ernesto is known to have made friends with them. But neither at school nor at university does he appear to have been in any real sense a political activist, preferring sport, reading, or playing chess to debating or direct action. Many years later in Cuba, Che himself declared: "I had no social preoccupations in my adolescence, and had no participation in the political or student struggles in Argentina."

What upheavals there were in the adolescent Ernesto's life took place much closer to home. He finished secondary school in Córdoba in December 1946 and found a job in a laboratory analyzing materials used for the construction of new roads in the province of Córdoba. Together with his friend Tomás Granado, he seems to have seen this as a good preparation for the degree in engineering he was intending to begin studying for in 1947. Yet before he could do so, several events occurred which produced a change of heart. His 98-year-old grandmother Ana became gravely ill in Buenos Aires, and he quit his job just in time to sit with her in her final illness. His parents also decided to return to live in the Argentine capital, although it soon became clear that they intended to live separately rather than as a family. Soon afterwards, Ernesto told them he had applied to study medicine, rather than engineering, at the University of Buenos Aires. After he became a leading member of the Cuban revolutionary government, he spoke of this decision:

> When I began to study medicine, I had few revolutionary concepts in my store-room of ideas. I wanted to succeed, as

everyone does. I dreamed of being a famous researcher, of working tirelessly to discover something which could eventually be made available to the whole of humanity, but which in the first instance represented a personal triumph. I was, as we all are, a product of my environment.

For the next three years, Ernesto was a reasonably diligent student at the Faculty of Medicine not far from his mother's house in central Buenos Aires. The house had been bought with funds that Che's father obtained when he finally sold the plantation up in Misiones. By now, he was no longer living with Celia, although the two had not divorced. This increased Ernesto's sense of responsibility as eldest son, and led to him seeking several part-time jobs while studying at the national university's medical school. Unlike many of his student colleagues, his studies were not interrupted by having to spend a year doing national service in the armed forces. For once, Che told his friends, "these shitty lungs have been useful for a change," although in the years to come he might have preferred to undergo military training in an orderly barracks rather than under fire in the Cuban mountains.

The faculty had the reputation of being one of the leading teaching schools in Latin America, and Ernesto attended lectures regularly, indulging in the usual medical student activities, including learning anatomy by fooling around with dead bodies. He found extra employment at the allergy clinic Clinica Pisani, run by Dr. Salvador Pisani, where he had first gone as a patient for his asthma, but was soon taken on as a research assistant and friend of the family. He made friends easily. He had several close women allies, ranging from his father's sister, his spinster Aunt Beatriz, who became a close confidante, to a student in his own year, Berta Gilda Infante, or "Tita," whom he wrote to for years even after he had left Argentina. As was usual for that time, most of his sexual experience seems to have been with maids and other women from a lower social class than his own, which was still bound by rigid conventions in sexual matters.

By the start of the 1950s, Ernesto was in his early twenties. As he studied and played, he was also anxious to explore more of Argentina. At the end of his third year of medicine, he set off on his first long journey of adventure. This was on a bicycle powered by a small motor—to help him up the hills. Ernesto wanted to discover the other side of Argentina: the northern provinces that rose to the Andes and were closer in population and spirit to the rest of South America. He called in first at Córdoba, where he saw his childhood friends, the Granado brothers. He spent several days visiting Alberto, who was older than him and was working in a leprosy hospital at nearby San Francisco del Chañar. Not only was this the start of a close friendship that was to last over many years, but it was also the beginning of his interest in illnesses carrying a social stigma with them, a sign that for the young Che medicine already had a strong ethical, if not political, component.

After Córdoba, Ernesto headed north, but not towards Misiones where had had spent his early childhood. Instead he traveled through some of the poorest parts of the country, Jujuy and Salta, inside the Tropic of Capricorn. He also biked through the province of Tucumán, where the conditions on the sugar plantations came closest to what he would experience years later during the revolutionary war in Cuba. (Two decades later, it was in Tucumán that idealistic young Argentines thought that the conditions of poverty and despair were such that it was here they could establish a Guevarist guerrilla *foco*—a revolutionary focus—that would rally the peasantry to their cause and help launch a revolution. But Argentina in the 1970s was not the Batista dictatorship of Cuba in the 1950s, and the would-be revolutionaries were soon wiped out or arrested.) Thoughts of revolution were still far from the young Ernesto's mind as he cycled through Tucumán and the other provinces, although he did begin to keep a diary in which he made increasingly critical observations about what he saw around him.

After six weeks of travel on his own, and having covered a distance of more than 2,500 miles, Ernesto returned for the start

Ernesto relaxing on his parents' balcony, Buenos Aires, 1949

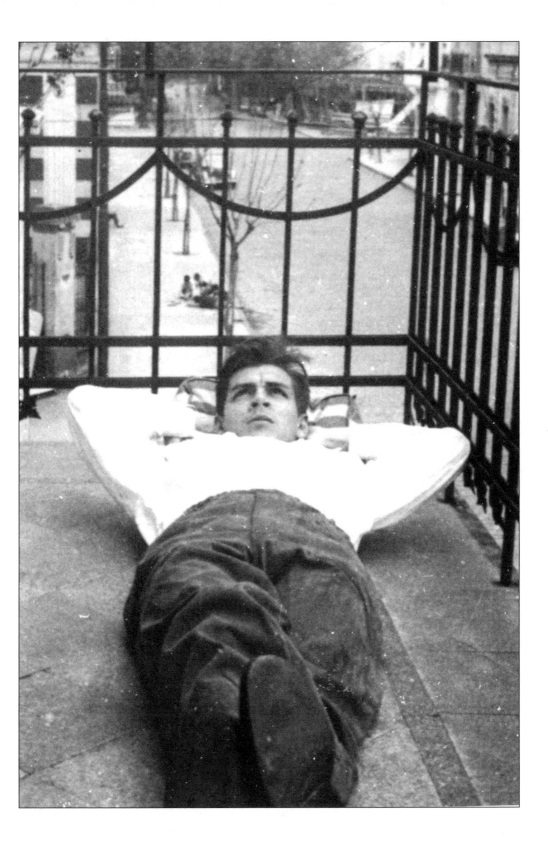

of his fourth year of medical studies. He even managed to earn himself a free overhaul of the bicycle, after writing a letter of recommendation to the manufacturers of the Cucchiolo engine that had helped power him around the Argentine interior.

Everyone who knew him in those days has stressed what a bohemian figure he was. Unlike most other middle-class Argentines then and now, he had little regard for his appearance, wearing the same shirt day after day, odd socks and occasionally even odd shoes. One of his nicknames was "El Chancho"—the Pig, and in terms of personal hygiene at least he seems to have lived up to the name. Yet his charm more than made up for any eccentricities, and this was what helped him when he met the first great love of his life. She was Maria del Carmen Ferreyra, known as "Chichina," and she was only sixteen. Her family was made up of landowners and industrialists in Córdoba, and although at first they found Ernesto amusing and different, they soon came down against him when he proposed marriage to the young girl. Chichina's cousin, Dolores Moyano, described Malagueño, the family estancia (ranch), and the incongruousness of the romance:

> [it] included two polo fields, Arab stallions, and a feudal village for the workers in the family's limestone quarries. The family visited the village church every Sunday for Mass, worshipping in a separate alcove to the right of the altar with its own entrance and private communion rail, away from the workers. In many ways, Malagueño exemplified everything Ernesto despised. Yet, unpredictable as always, Ernesto had fallen in love with the princess of this little empire, my cousin Chichina Ferreyra, an extraordinarily beautiful and charming girl, who, to the dismay of her parents, was equally fascinated by Ernesto.

This romantic involvement did not dampen his wanderlust. At the end of the university year in 1950, Ernesto signed on as a doctor on merchant ships owned by the Argentine state oil firm, YPF. Over the next few months he visited the coast of South America from Trinidad in the Caribbean to Comodoro Rivadavia in the south of Argentina. In letters to his family, Ernesto expressed his disappointment at the fact that the ships spent all their time at sea and only a few hours in port, which gave him no chance to see or get to know anything of life in the rest of the continent. He put the hours of inactivity to good use, reading as ever, and writing. It is from this period that his first known short story, called "Anguish," dates. It is melodramatic stuff, and ends with the lament: "To make a sterile sacrifice that does nothing to create a new life... that is anguish."

These seagoing adventures lasted only a few months. In June 1950 he was back on land in Buenos Aires, where he took more exams, passing them as he had always done. But by this time, Ernesto was tiring of life as a medical student; what he had glimpsed of Latin America outside Argentina held a much greater attraction. His opportunity to explore it at closer quarters came thanks to his friend, the leprosy expert Alberto Granado, in Córdoba. Granado, by this time nearing thirty, had been talking about traveling through South America by motorbike for many years. Now his enthusiastic younger friend pushed him to take the plunge, to embark on a journey intended to stretch from Chile in the south right up to the United States.

The two men set off from Buenos Aires on January 4, 1952 on board *La Poderosa II* (The Mighty One), a vintage British Norton 500cc bike. They first spent several days at Miramar, the upper-class Atlantic seabord resort where Chichina was enjoying her summer vacation. Ernesto asked his young fiancée to wait for him; she gave him fifteen dollars to buy her a swimming costume when he reached the United States. Then Alberto and Ernesto began their adventure for real.

They headed south, to Patagonia and the Andes. While they were still in Argentina, a "Dear Ernesto" letter caught up with them. Chichina told him baldly that their romance was over. According to Ernesto's *Notas de viaje* (translated as *The Motorcycle Diaries*), "I read and reread the incredible letter. Just like that, all my dreams came crashing down." This did not mean that he turned back, however, and soon he and Alberto had crossed from Argentina into Chile.

*On December 29, 1951, Guevara (center) and his friend Alberto Granado
climb onto an old Norton 500: the start of a trip across Latin America*

As his Notas de viaje show, this journey was what first really
opened Ernesto's eyes to the depth of the social problems
afflicting Latin America. The 2004 film *The Motorcycle Diaries*,
directed by Walter Salles, presents this awakening of Che's
social conscience as a more or less straightforward process, but
the diaries themselves are a much more chaotic expression of

everything that he saw and felt during the journey of adventure. What the film does capture, however, is the sense of how in many ways, Argentina was a country set apart from the rest of the continent. It was comparatively rich and developed, and with a thriving, well-educated middle class to which the Guevara family belonged.

The composition of its people was also quite different from other Latin American countries, especially those further north and in the Caribbean. For a start, there were no black Argentines. Although in the eighteenth century there had been an influx of black slaves from Africa, in Argentina there had never been the concentrated plantation system that had existed in Brazil or the Caribbean. Many of the slave descendants died in the wars of independence, intermarried, or moved across the Rio de la Plata to the larger colonies of black people in Uruguay. By the end of the nineteenth century, there is no further record of significant groups of black Argentines.

Nor was there the concentration of indigenous people in Argentina that Ernesto met in the north of Chile and Peru: apart from during his earlier bicycle ride through the northern provinces of his country, Ernesto's only contact with this integral part of the continent's peoples was through maids and laborers in the cities. It was only when he traveled through Peru and saw them as an excluded majority (in Peru many of the highland Aymara and Quechua-speaking groups still lived in feudal conditions that had changed little since the days of Spanish colonial rule) that he began to appreciate the inequalities of life for millions of Latin Americans.

This inequality was brought home to him when he saw for himself the conditions in the mines of Chile. By the time he and Alberto visited the huge copper mines in northern Chile near Antofagasta, they had emerged unscathed from many picaresque adventures, including a failed attempt to get to Easter Island, where they hoped to combine a visit to a leper colony with the charms of the local women, who they were told were crazy for white men. They managed to drag the Norton as far as the Chilean capital, Santiago, before it finally gave out. This did not dampen the two travelers' enthusiasm to continue on up the continent to the United States. In the north of Chile, they then used their medical credentials to obtain permission to visit the giant Chuquicamata copper mine. Ernesto was predictably horrified by the conditions of the workers there, and had what seems to have been his first experience of meeting a communist militant. The Chilean government had banned the Communist Party in 1948, and the communist miner had been imprisoned for three months. Ernesto saw him and his wife as the "living representation of the proletariat in any part of the world," but plainly did not know as yet what to make of communism. In his diary he wrote:

> It's a great pity that they repress people like this. Apart from whether collectivism, the "communist vermin," is a danger to decent life, the communism gnawing at his entrails was no more than a natural longing for something better, a protest against persistent hunger transformed into a love for this strange doctrine, whose essence he could never grasp but whose translation, "bread for the poor," was something he understood and, more importantly, that filled him with hope.

The Chuquicamata mine also seems to have been the first time he came into contact with the gringos who ran the copper industry, whom he dismisses as cold, calculating exploiters. Faced with this stark evidence of capitalist exploitation, he ends this section of the diary wondering whether such soul-destroying work as mining can ever be undertaken joyfully. He concludes with a sentence revealing that he is not yet convinced that communism is the answer: "They say that's what it's like over there, where the red blaze that now lights up the world comes from. So they say. I don't know."

Alberto and Ernesto then trekked through the deserts of northern Chile into the south of Peru, heading for the old Inca capital, Cusco. Ernesto's diary, full of sweeping reflections on history as well as their day-to-day adventures, becomes especially lyrical when he sees what the Incas called the "navel of the world." Trying in his travel notes to play the role of the detached, knowledgeable observer, he considers Cusco in three ways. The first of these is his vision of the Incas, whose way of life was destroyed by Spanish *conquistadores*. He is also aware of the *mestizo* civilization that has been created over the four centuries since that European conquest, and admires the "vibrant city whose monuments bear witness to the formidable courage of the warriors who conquered the region in the name of Spain." What he is most doubtful about is the tourist view of the Andean world, which reduces any experience to a superficial, meaningless snapshot of a world the casual visitor is excluded from. This distaste for tourists and their shallow vision of Latin American civilizations came to the fore after a trip to the ruins of Machu Picchu, where he derided in particular those North Americans who "fly direct to Lima, tour Cusco, visit the ruins and return straight home, not believing that anything else is worth seeing."

Ernesto obviously saw himself as far more involved with the landscapes and people he was seeing at first hand, even if he and Alberto were relatively privileged as white Argentine "doctors." The Argentine explorers soon headed for Lima themselves, where Ernesto was able to recover from his bouts of asthma and where they were cordially received by the Peruvian leprosy expert Dr. Hugo Pesce. This local authority greatly impressed the young Che—his devotion to the cause of doing good in society was the kind of selfless activity guaranteed to appeal to the idealistic young Argentine. Several years later, when he wrote his first book about the revolutionary war in Cuba, he remembered the good doctor and sent him a copy. Doctor Pesce also helped the two young medics return to their original idea of visiting and working in leprosy hospitals. By now they had in any case given up on the plan of reaching the United States; their means of transport had long since gone, and they were finding it increasingly difficult to raise funds, while the tiredness of continually being on the road seemed to be taking its toll with Ernesto's illness. So they now headed to the San Pablo leper colony run by Dr. Pesce in the Amazon region in the east of Peru, close to its border with Brazil and Colombia.

After more adventures on the river boat from Pucallpa to the leper colony, Ernesto and Alberto arrived more or less unscathed at San Pablo in June 1952. They immediately impressed the staff and the 600 patients who were kept in the lepers' compound by their willingness to mix with the sufferers, shaking hands with them without any gloves or other protection, eating and playing football with them, and generally treating them as normal human beings. They spent two weeks at the hospital, during which time Che took the opportunity to swim the Amazon, almost half a mile wide at this point, while Alberto was confirmed in his desire to work more with leprosy.

On June 14, 1952, Ernesto's twenty-fourth birthday, patients and medical staff threw him a party. In his reply to a toast in his honor, he for perhaps the first time clearly, if somewhat drunkenly, expressed the kind of pan-Latin Americanism that was to be one of his guiding principles:

> Although our insignificance means we can't be spoke-speople for such a noble cause, we believe, and after this journey more firmly than ever, that the division of America into unstable and illusory nations is completely fictional. We constitute a single mestizo race, which from Mexico to the Magellan Straits bears notable ethnographical similarities. And so, in an attempt to rid myself of the weight of small-minded provincialism, I propose a toast to Peru and to a United Latin America.

The hospital staff presented him and Alberto with a wooden raft for them to be able to continue their journey down the Amazon. They baptized it the *Mambo-Tango*, probably because of Ernesto's complete inability to distinguish between any dance rhythms, a failing which had caused him huge embarrassment and Alberto great amusement throughout their trip. Their original intention was to sail this unwieldy craft all the way down to the city of Manaus in Brazil, famous for its opera house in the midst of the jungle, and from there to travel by river up to Venezuela. After three days of struggling with the Amazon's currents and clouds of mosquitoes, however, the two explorers decided instead to seek the safety of the town of Leticia, perched on the river's edge in Colombia, at the border between all three countries.

Here they found perhaps the most lucrative employment of their entire trip. Although Che had played rugby at school, and Alberto was no great expert either, the fact that they came from Argentina meant only one thing for the locals: they must be expert soccer players. Their imaginary talents soon came to the ears of the manager of the Independiente Sporting de Leticia club, which was struggling to make an impression in the local league. The two young Argentines were immediately employed to train the first team, and to play in it themselves: Ernesto became the goalkeeper, Alberto was one of the crack forwards. Surprisingly enough, their training seems to have brought results (or so Che boasted in his diaries). They reached the final of a cup competition and (again according to Che) got as far as a penalty shootout. He himself saved one of the opponents' penalty attempts, but the Independiente strikers missed them all.

After this moment of near-glory, Alberto and Ernesto decided it was time to move on.

After seven months on the road, their final destination was the Venezuelan capital, Caracas. This involved them in a flight in a military plane out of Leticia, followed by a short, uneasy stopover in Bogotá, the capital of Colombia, where the tensions of a civil war that has lasted from the 1950s to the present day were already making themselves felt. From Bogotá they traveled by bus and truck to Caracas. Alberto had a letter of recommendation from the kind Dr. Pesce, and was taken on immediately as a doctor in a leprosy clinic. Ernesto, who unlike his friend had not yet finished his medical degree, decided it was time to return to Buenos Aires, with the intention of coming back a year later to rejoin his companion.

While in the Venezuelan capital, he wrote of the slums on the hills all around the glittering center of the city; his descriptions of the indolent poor blacks living there, compared to more recent, dynamic and wealthier Portuguese immigrants, show to what extent, despite his declarations of finding common cause with the poor of Latin America, he was still completely bound up with his white, privileged middle-class Argentine background. Ironically however, before he got back to Buenos Aires, Ernesto was treated to his first glimpse of the country for which he had already expressed such dislike. One of his uncles was a racehorse breeder, who shipped horses from Buenos Aires to Miami via Caracas. Ernesto hitched a ride in the plane with his uncle and horses, and at the end of July 1952 found himself in Miami. Due to lengthy repairs on the aircraft, what had originally been meant as a stopover of only a few days turned into a stay of almost three weeks. Sharing with a cousin of Chichina, he lived the kind of hand-to-mouth existence he had become so expert at during his long journey, but his diary contains no great insights or analysis of what he thought of the "giant of the north."

Ernesto eventually returned by plane to Buenos Aires in August 1952. Over the next few months, in what was to become a habitual way of writing, he wrote up an extended version of his travel diaries. They give a remarkably honest insight into the social and political education of a young Argentine seeing the reality of a continent for the first time. Although some of the descriptions are trite, revealing what he has read rather than his own lived experience, his narrative skills at relating the comic as well as darker moments and incidents of his travels are already well developed.

The diary was not made public until many years later, however, and the first writing published under his name (as one of the authors) was the unlikely "Sensibilization of Guinea Pigs to Pollens through Injections of Orange Extract." This article appeared in the scientific journal *Alergia* at the end of 1951, and shows that by now he was one of Dr. Pisani's leading assistants.

In addition to his writing, Ernesto still had to pass almost half the medical exams required before he could qualify as a doctor from Buenos Aires University. After applying himself steadily for several months, he finally received his diploma in June 1953, shortly before his twenty-fifth birthday. Yet if his family were hoping that he might now settle down to a comfortable professional existence in Argentina, making use of his degree, they were immediately disappointed. Ernesto was still keen to meet up again with Alberto Granado, and to continue their adventure up to the United States, or to work in Venezuela rather than in Argentina.

This time his companion was another childhood friend from Córdoba, Carlos "Calica" Ferrer. The two of them planned the journey slightly more thoroughly than on the previous occasion, milking as many relatives as possible for money, and setting out by train rather than on a motorbike. Ernesto's family came to see him off at Belgrano station on the long journey up to La Paz in Bolivia. His mother Celia is said to have run along the platform, despairing of ever seeing her son again. Although, happily, this was not to be the case, when they did meet again, Ernesto had become "Che" Guevara, and was no longer uncertain of his destiny.

2
MEETING HIS DESTINY
(1953–1956)

At the age of twenty-five, Ernesto Guevara began his second long trip outside Argentina. The first journey had shown him to be increasingly aware of social conditions around him, as well as conscious of all that he had to learn about life in the rest of the continent. This second voyage changed his life completely, turning him from an intellectually curious medical doctor into one of the future leaders of the revolution in Cuba.

After several days' travel through Argentina's northern deserts and the Bolivian altiplano, the first port of call he and "Calica" Ferrer made was in La Paz. Projecting backwards from his untimely death in Bolivia fourteen years later, some writers have seen the month he spent in Bolivia in 1953 as his "Damascene" moment, the occasion when his eyes were fully opened to the horrors of capitalist exploitation, and his commitment to change through communist revolution was born. From his letters and the comments of Ferrer and others he met at the time, it seems wishful thinking to conclude that this experience was crucial in forming Ernesto's revolutionary credo. His glimpse of the nationalist revolution led by President Victor Paz Estenssoro was, however, another important step in his political development.

The Bolivian "revolution" had begun a year earlier, when the government of the Nationalist Revolutionary Movement had swept into power on the back of popular uprisings. One of the new government's first steps had been to nationalize the privately-held mines of tin and other metals, which were the main source of Bolivia's wealth. Pushed to carry out this nationalization policy by the powerful miner's union led by Juan Lechín, President Paz Estenssoro was more cautious about taking the further step of reforming land ownership, which, then as now, was seen as a vital key to guaranteeing greater justice and equality. The first moves towards this land reform were planned for August 2, 1953, when the two young Argentines were in the Bolivian capital.

In fact, Ernesto missed the mass demonstrations that accompanied these reforms. He was visiting a mine outside the capital, with a view to possibly finding employment there. As at Chuquicamata on his earlier trip, the conditions he caught a glimpse of at the Bolsa Negra wolframite mine convinced him once more that the nationalization process needed to be taken much further in order to bring real change to the miners' lives. He and Alberto went deep underground, and Guevara could not help but be impressed by the atmosphere inside the mine, some seventeen thousand feet up in the Andes. "The silence weighs on even those who like us are not able to speak its language," he wrote. The visit to the mine also convinced him that Latin American countries such as Bolivia or Chile had to reduce their dependency on exports of raw materials to the United States: "It is the only thing that keeps Bolivia going. It is a mineral the Americans buy, and that is why the Bolivian government has ordered an increase in production."

Ernesto and Calica also saw how split Bolivian society was, not so much on political as on racial grounds. In one famous incident, the two young men were visiting the newly formed Ministry for Peasant Affairs, when they were horrified to see that all the Quechua-speaking Indians who came into the building were being fumigated with DDT. When they questioned the minister they had come to see about what they had witnessed, he replied matter-of-factly that the Indians were covered in lice, and that until the government could improve educational standards in the country and teach them about hygiene, there was nothing for it but to adopt this kind of precautionary measure. Calica seems to have accepted this argument, but for Ernesto (according at least to Ricardo Rojo), it was crucial to change this kind of attitude:

> This revolution will fail unless it succeeds in breaking through the Indians' spiritual isolation, touching them to the core, shaking them to their very bones, giving them back their stature as human beings. Otherwise, what good is it?

Ricardo Rojo was a lawyer who associated with a group of rich Argentines who had fled Perón in Argentina, and whom Ernesto and Calica soon got to know in the Bolivian capital. Rojo was to pop up several times subsequently on Ernesto's journey, and to become a close friend. After almost a month in Bolivia, the desire to push on north led the two travelers to agree to leave Bolivia behind, despite the interest Ernesto showed in the unfolding political events. As on the earlier trip, the next stop was Peru and in particular Machu Picchu and the ancient Inca capital of Cusco. This once again brought out the amateur archaeologist in Che, but his traveling companion was less enamored of the dirt and squalor he discovered all around him in the Andean highlands. When the pair finally found their way to the capital Lima, and could, as far as their meagre budget would permit, enjoy the comforts of modern city life, Ferrer wrote a relieved, thankful letter to his mother back in Argentina.

In Lima they were welcomed once again by Dr. Pesce, but were made to feel less welcome by the border police and their colleagues in the Peruvian capital. At the border, Ernesto had some books on the Bolivian revolution and on life in Soviet Russia confiscated. In Lima, their hotel rooms were searched for more "subversive" propaganda.

These unwelcome interventions undoubtedly helped the two adventurers decide it was time to move on up the coast to Ecuador, although their final destination was still Venezuela. They spent several weeks becalmed in the tropical port city of Guayaquil. Ernesto was recovering from several bad bouts of asthma, and they shared lodgings with other young Argentines traveling through the continent. At some point during his stay in the Ecuadorean port city, Ernesto changed his mind about meeting up with Alberto Granado in Caracas, and instead resolved to go with his new companions to the largest Central American country, Guatemala. Calica Ferrer, meanwhile, chose to stick with their original plan, and went on to Quito, and from there to Venezuela, where he met up with Alberto Granado and was to live for the next ten years.

Together with Gualo García, one of his new-found Argentine friends, Ernesto eventually set off from Ecuador on an Argentine cargo boat bound for Central America. After a short stopover in Panama, where he had his first journalistic success, selling two stories from his earlier journey around South America, by the end of November 1953 they had reached Costa Rica. This small Central American country was a rare functioning democracy among the dictatorships of the rest of the isthmus.

Under the leadership of President José Figueres, Costa Rica had abolished its army, nationalized the banking system and yet not alienated the North Americans. It was an oasis of calm in the region, and as such attracted not merely Argentine adventurers but democratic exiles from all over the region as well as the Caribbean. During the days he spent in the capital San José, Ernesto is known to have had long conversations with both Rómulo Betancourt from Venezuela and Juan Bosch, who had fled a Caribbean dictator, Leonidas Trujillo of the Dominican Republic. His opinion of the former Venezuelan president, who had been kicked out of his country by the military, was less than enthusiastic, describing him as "a politician with a few fixed ideas in his head, but with everything else malleable to fit in with whatever best suits him." Juan Bosch, the writer and leader of the exiled Dominican Revolutionary Party, who was to play a leading role in the history of his country for the next half century, made a much more favorable impression: "He is a literary man of clear ideas and of a clearly leftist tendency. We didn't speak of literature [Guevara still plainly considered himself a budding writer], simply of politics."

Ernesto also met other figures who had found exile in Costa Rica after failing to overthrow a dictator. In San José he met Calixto García and Severino Rosell, survivors of the first concerted attack on the Batista regime: the assault on the Moncada barracks in Santiago, the second city of Cuba, on July 26, 1953. The attack had been commanded by a prominent student leader, one Fidel Castro Ruz. The assault had failed, and Castro and his mainly youthful combatants were rounded up soon afterwards. The first 61 prisoners were tortured and shot, but Fidel was luckier, and was able to defend himself in court, where he pronounced one of his most famous phrases: "History will absolve me." He was sentenced to fifteen years in jail on the Isla de los Pinos along with several others, while a few survivors of the organization were able to escape to Costa Rica and other Central American countries.

It was from Costa Rica in November 1953 that Ernesto wrote a letter to his Aunt Beatriz back in Buenos Aires that has become famous as one of his most polemical missives. Referring to what he had seen of the estates run by the US-owned United Fruit Company in Panama and on board one of their cargo boats, he wrote to his aunt that "passing through the dominions of the United Fruit has convinced me yet again of how terrible these capitalist octopuses are. I swore in front of a portrait of the late lamented comrade Stalin that I would not rest until those octopuses had been slain…" Those who see Che Guevara as a bloodthirsty Stalinist take this threat literally, and are convinced that even this early in his career, the Argentine revolutionary was bent on taking up arms to destroy the capitalist order, whatever the cost. Others, probably more sensibly, see the letter as poking fun at his aunt and her tendency to see "reds under the beds" at every turn, although the letter ends on a new-found tone of determination: "In Guatemala, I will perfect myself and achieve what I need to be a true revolutionary." He signed off with: "from your nephew of the iron constitution, empty stomach and unquenchable faith in the socialist future."

Shortly afterwards, Ernesto and Gualo García crossed into Nicaragua, where they met up again with Ricardo Rojo and two other Argentines, heading south. Ernesto succeeded in hitching a ride, and on Christmas Eve 1953, drove into Guatemala City. Like Bolivia, Guatemala in 1953 was in the throes of a nationalist revolution. Unlike Bolivia, it was relatively close to the United States and had huge US economic interests, mostly concerning the United Fruit Company. Its three million inhabitants were deeply divided, with the indigenous majority of Mayan descent excluded from wealth, politics and land ownership. Most of them worked on huge latifundios or agricultural estates run by descendants of the Spanish conquerors, or on the banana, coffee and cotton plantations controlled by the all-powerful United Fruit Company. The company owners were incensed at the moderate reform measures brought in by the Guatemalan president, Jacobo Arbenz Guzmán, after he had emerged victorious at a rare free election in 1951. Among the laws his government passed were those establishing a minimum wage, the right to strike and collective bargaining. President Arbenz also continued with attempts at agrarian reform aimed at the expropriation of latifundios with absentee landlords, and the break-up of some monopolies. The United Fruit Company's owners, many of whom had close links to the Eisenhower administration in Washington, were quick to denounce all this as communism run wild.

At the same time, Arbenz's progressive program attracted hundreds of left-leaning intellectuals from the rest of Latin America and the Caribbean. One of them, a Peruvian woman called Hilda Gadea, was to have a profound influence on Ernesto not only during the eight months he spent in Guatemala, but also in Mexico, where the couple were eventually married and had a daughter. Hilda Gadea was a militant in the banned Peruvian APRA (People's Revolutionary Alliance of America) party, a movement almost as diverse as Peronism in Ernesto's native Argentina. Hilda was three and a half years older than he was, and much more widely read. She had participated actively in political struggles in Peru as well as in Guatemala, but she was not a convinced Marxist. From the first moment she met Ernesto, she seems to have played the role of mother and provider—she stood guarantee for his rent, supplied him with food and books to read, argued and fought with him over ideas of revolution and representative democracy. There was also a strong romantic attachment, although Ernesto never admitted to being as attached to her as he claimed she was to him.

It was after his Argentine friends left in February 1954 that the two of them were increasingly thrown together. Soon afterwards she was shocked to discover him in the midst of an acute asthma attack.

> It was at that moment I fully realized what his illness meant. I could not help admiring his strength of character and his self-discipline… Trying to conceal how much I had been touched by all of this, I talked about everything and nothing, all the while thinking what a shame it was that a man of such worth, who could do so much for society, who was so intelligent and generous, had to suffer such an affliction; if I were in his place I would shoot myself. I decided there and then to stick by him.

After this experience she not only helped him through his bouts of asthma, but paid his bills, cooked and generally fussed over him. For his part, Che was not always so gallant. In March he recorded in his diary:

> Hilda declared her love in epistolary and practical form. I was feeling very bad with asthma, otherwise I might have made love to her. I warned her that all I could offer her was a casual contact, nothing definitive. She seemed very put out. The short letter she left me when she went is very good. Too bad she is so ugly. She is twenty-seven.

In addition to Hilda, Ernesto was able to discuss Latin American politics with the hundreds of other political exiles drawn to Guatemala at the start of 1954. There were Argentines who opposed Perón, Peruvians, opponents of the dictatorships in El Salvador and Nicaragua, and more Cubans opposed to the Batista regime. Ernesto became friends above all with "Ñico" López, a student who had been involved in an attack on another army barracks in Cuba. After the failure of the assault, he had taken refuge in the Guatemalan embassy in that country, and ended up in Guatemala City. Apart from anything else, López seems to have been the first person to baptize Ernesto Guevara de la Serna with the nickname "Che." The two men were involved in several harebrained schemes to make money, including selling images of Our Lord of Esquipulas, the figure of a black Christ held in popular veneration throughout Guatemala.

Apart from these continuing efforts to make ends meet, Ernesto was as anxious as ever to pursue his medical career. He soon found that the Guatemalan bureaucracy was as hard to overcome as any system in Central America, and none of the promised positions resulted in any steady work. He also began to plan an ambitious book, entitled *The Role of the Doctor in Latin America*, which he returned to on many occasions both here and in Mexico, although it never got much further than the planning stage. By now, the political situation in Guatemala was reaching crisis point. The CIA had been arming and training an "army of liberation" across the border in Honduras, and only four days after Ernesto's 26th birthday in June 1954, these forces, led by Colonel Carlos Castillo Armas, began their invasion of Guatemala. Arbenz soon discovered that he did not have the support of his own military, and on June 27, 1954 the generals forced him to resign. Castillo Armas flew into Guatemala City triumphantly on July 3rd, accompanied by the US ambassador.

This experience marked Ernesto deeply. He had been convinced that President Arbenz would fight the invaders, writing to his mother: "Without a doubt Colonel Arbenz is a guy with guts, and is ready to die at his post if need be." His actual experience of the fighting seems to have been that of the wide-eyed tourist:

> ... even the lightest bombings raids look majestic. I saw one plane aiming for a target relatively close to where I was, and you could see the plane growing larger and larger while tongues of flame shot out from its wings, and hear the sound of its machine guns and the lighter anti-aircraft guns firing back. All at once the plane hung in the air, then it plunged downwards and you could feel the earth tremble when the bomb hit.

Despite assertions by his Cuban biographers that he played an active part in defending President Arbenz's democratic govern-ment, the most Ernesto seems to have done was to sign up for a volunteer medical team to help with casualties. His skills were never called on, as President Arbenz refused all calls to hand out weapons to the people and confront his opponents militarily. When Arbenz was ousted, Ernesto concluded that might had to be fought with might. He wrote to his childhood friend Tita Infante back in Argentina that the Arbenz government should have defended itself by carrying out "a certain number of executions" in order to protect itself.

Immediately after the coup, martial law was declared, and Communist Party members and sympathisers were rounded up. As a known political activist, Hilda was picked up, questioned for several days, and then released. While she was in custody, Ernesto sought political asylum along with more than a hundred others in the Argentine embassy. After several weeks, President Perón sent a plane to evacuate all those Argentines who wanted to be repatriated, but Ernesto had no desire to return to Buenos Aires, especially as it might seem that his latest venture into the world outside Argentina had ended in defeat. Instead, he chose to carry on north to Mexico, where the deposed President Arbenz and many of the other Latin American exiles also chose to go.

Mexico had long been a country that welcomed exiles. After its own agrarian revolution had finally become institutionalized in the early 1930s, successive governments of the PRI (the Institutional Revolutionary Party) had not only made sure their country's foreign policy was as independent as possible from that of the United States, but had welcomed exiles from Europe and the rest of Latin America. These varied from Leon Trotsky to the leaders of the defeated Spanish Republic, as well as many intellectuals, writers and artists. Similarly, opponents of the dictators of the small Central American countries naturally gravitated to the much larger and more open capital of Mexico to regroup and reorganize.

Ernesto Guevara arrived in Mexico City in late September 1954. It was to be his home for more than two years. As usual, he had little money, no idea of what work, if any, he could do, and only a few contacts in Mexico supplied by his family and people he had met during his nine months in Guatemala. His experience of the failure of President Arbenz's government in the face of pressure from the United States and international business interests had by now made him a fervent anti-imperialist. Over the next few months, the new friends he made in the Mexican capital would not only help turn him into a convinced communist, but give him the opportunity to put his revolutionary beliefs immediately to the test in Cuba.

First, as ever, the twenty-six-year-old Guevara had to find work. He bought himself a camera and started taking portraits in Mexico City parks and at birthday parties. According to friends, his Argentine accent made the mothers of the children he photographed laugh so much that they nearly always bought his snapshots. At the same time, thanks to his Argentine medical qualifications, he was given an intern's position on the allergy ward at the Mexico City General Hospital. It was here that he again ran into someone in a meeting that probably changed his destiny. His Cuban friend Ñico López brought a fellow countryman into the hospital suffering from an allergy, and though he himself soon returned to Cuba, he put Guevara in touch with the small group of Cuban exiles who had been ordered to reassemble in Mexico after the failure of the attack on the Moncada barracks. Another significant re-encounter from Guatemala was with the Peruvian political activist Hilda Gadea. She had finally been deported from Guatemala in November 1954, and the first thing she did when she reached Mexico City was to call Ernesto. According to her later version of events, the Argentine immediately proposed marriage, but when she hesitated because she had still not found her feet in this new environment, he grew impatient and suggested instead that they should just be "good friends." Their relationship continued in this on-off way for many months, until a dramatic event changed it completely.

In the meantime, Ernesto seemed to be happy working once more as a doctor specializing in allergies. As usual he was reading an enormous amount, from Pablo Neruda's poetry to social realist novels and more rigorous economic and political handbooks, many of them Marxist. Early in 1955, his job as a photographer also received a boost when he was appointed official photographer for the Agencia Latina agency at the Panamerican Games then being held in Mexico City. The Agencia Latina was an "independent" news agency set up by President Perón to challenge what he saw as the distorted view of Argentina and Latin America given by the developed world's news agencies. Although the initiative collapsed in 1955 even before Perón was ousted, there is little doubt that it provided the germ of an idea that was to flourish later in revolutionary Cuba when Che Guevara set up the Prensa Latina news agency.

In June 1955 his relationship with that Caribbean island and in particular with those who were trying to overthrow the Batista regime there took a dramatic turn. It was then that he met Raúl, the younger of the Castro brothers. Raúl had been forced to flee Cuba after the Batista government issued a warrant for his arrest. He sought refuge in the Mexican Embassy, and was flown to Mexico on June 24. Ernesto Guevara was among the group of exiles living in the Mexican capital whom Raúl met as soon as he arrived, and Ernesto invited him over to Hilda's flat for a meal. The Argentine did not record their first meeting in any of his diaries, but Hilda was immediately impressed: "his ideas were very clear as to how the revolution was to be made, and more importantly, for what purpose and for whom." From then on, the two men began to meet several times a week, and their conversations seem to have pushed Ernesto further along the path towards accepting that a communist revolution was the answer to freeing the Caribbean and Latin America from US dominance.

This new friendship was followed in July by an even more important one: that of Fidel Castro himself. Imprisoned after the Moncada attack, Fidel had also benefited from an amnesty, and for a while had attempted to continue his political activities in Havana. Before many weeks had passed, however, he became convinced it was too dangerous to stay on the island. Equipped with a tourist visa for Mexico, he left Cuba on the afternoon of July 7, 1955. He left a parting message for his supporters:

> I am leaving Cuba because all chance of a peaceful resistance has been closed to me. Six weeks after being released from prison I am more sure than ever of the dictator's deter-mination to remain in power, ruling by the use of terror and crime... I believe the hour has come to demand our rights and not beg for them, to fight for them instead of pleading for them. I will temporarily make my home somewhere in the Caribbean. From journeys such as this, a man either does not return or else returns with the tyranny dismembered at his feet.

This kind of grandiloquence was bound to appeal to the young Argentine, desperate for a noble cause in which to enlist. One evening, shortly after his arrival in the Mexican capital, Fidel Castro, Raúl and Ernesto went out together for a meal. According to eyewitnesses, at this first meeting the three of them talked all night about their vision of Latin America, the international situation and the possibilities of revolution. Fidel explained his plans to return and oust Batista, and invited the Argentine to join them as the group's doctor. Ernesto signed up immediately, and was sufficiently impressed to write in his diary: "One political event is to have met Fidel Castro, the Cuban revolutionary, an intelligent young man who is very sure of himself and very audacious; I think we both liked each other." Meanwhile, events on another front required more attention from Ernesto. At the start of August 1955, Hilda announced that she was pregnant. In his diary the father-to-be was less than romantic about the news: "Someone else might consider this transcendental, to me it is an uncomfortable episode. I'm going to have a child, and am getting married to Hilda in a few days."

Thanks to the impenetrable Mexican bureaucracy, the few days stretched to a fortnight, so that it was not until August 18, 1955 that the pair were married in the small town of Tepot-zotlán, to the north of Mexico City. Raúl Castro was present at the wedding; Fidel came to the party afterwards. The pair informed their parents after the event, Ernesto only including the news as a postscript in a letter to his mother more than a month later. "I'm sending you the news officially for you to distribute: I have married Hilda Gadea and we will shortly be having a child."

It was only a couple of months later that the pair took their honeymoon, traveling to the Yucatán peninsula where Ernesto once more indulged his passion for archaeology by exploring the Mayan ruins of Uxmal and Chichen Itza. Coming back, they took a boat along the coast of the Gulf of Mexico, little realizing that only a year later Ernesto would be setting out again across the same waters with a very different purpose.

By now his main passion was the dream of making a revolution in Cuba. Fidel Castro returned to Mexico after a successful fundraising trip in the United States and declared that 1956 was to be the year when he and his men would make the great breakthrough in their fight against Batista: "In 1956 we will be free or we will be martyrs," was his pledge. The Cuban exiles who saw Fidel as their leader began to gather in different parts of Mexico, and physical and weapons training started. The gymnastics were led by a famous Mexican wrestler, "Kid" Vanegas. For shooting practice Fidel rented the premises of a rifle club on the outskirts of the capital. Later, Fidel recruited a one-eyed Cuban colonel who had fought with the Republicans in Spain to teach his men all he knew about guerrilla tactics. The makeshift guerrillas were far from being a disciplined squad, but what they lacked in professionalism they made up for in revolutionary ardor.

In the midst of this training for guerrilla combat, Ernesto Guevara became a father. His daughter, Hilda Beatriz, was born in the English Hospital in Mexico City on February 15, 1956. Far from raising any doubts as to whether he should be undertaking such a foolhardy adventure as his plan to join the Cuban revolutionaries, his daughters' birth seems to have done just the opposite. He wrote in his dairy:

> the birth gives me a double reason for joy. First, because it puts a stop to a disastrous marital situation, and second because I am now absolutely sure that I can leave, in spite of everything. My inability to live with her mother is even greater than the affection with which I look on her. For a while I was worried that a combination of my delight with the child and consideration for her mother (who in many ways is a fine woman, and who loves me in an almost unhealthy way) would end up turning me into the boring father of a family... but now I know this isn't so.

By May 1956 the would-be revolutionaries went into full-time training on a ranch they had hired in Chalco, some fifty miles east of the capital. Ernesto gave up his job at the General

Hospital and his medical research work, and said goodbye to Hilda. When Fidel appointed him to be in charge of one of the guerrillas' safe houses, some of the Cubans expressed misgivings that a foreigner had been made their leader. Fidel immediately quashed their objections, emphasizing that Che's commitment to the revolution in Cuba was all the more remarkable as he had not been born there or suffered under the repressive Batista regime. This argument apparently smoothed the matter over, and from then on none of the Cubans questioned the man known as "Che," especially as it was plain that he was always demanding more of himself than the rest of them. At the end of their training, "Colonel" Bayo reported that he was the best of them all.

Che responded to Fidel's confidence in him in many ways. He even wrote a sub-Pablo Neruda Ode to Fidel: "Let's go/ardent prophet of dawn/along hidden, unfenced paths/to free the green crocodile you love so much." He also joined in the lengthy discussions held between the exiles about what kind of revolution they were hoping to bring to the "green crocodile" that is Cuba. The July 26 Movement that Fidel Castro led (named after the day of the attack on the Moncada barracks) was by no means monolithically Marxist—some of the would-be guerrillas just wanted to get rid of Batista in order to take power themselves, whereas only a few such as Raúl Castro were convinced that the revolution they were about to launch had to be socialist if it were to succeed. Che Guevara had enough respect for the Castro brothers and the other Cubans not to try to impose his beliefs on them, but to trust that they could make a revolution successfully, and then ensure that it embodied the socialist ideals he was increasingly espousing.

This period of training and debate was rudely interrupted towards the end of June 1956. First Fidel, Hilda, and other members of the Cuban exile group were picked up by the police in Mexico City. Then the police went out to the ranch at Chalco and detained the rest, except for Raúl. They were put in the Miguel Schultz detention center while the authorities

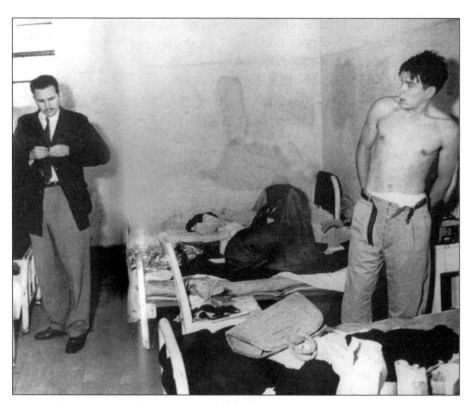

Fidel Castro (left) and Che in the Miguel Schultz detention center, Mexico

decided what to do with them: should they be deported back to Cuba, tried for political activities which foreigners were not allowed to engage in while in Mexico, or set free as opponents of an oppressive regime? Unlike the others, what Ernesto most feared was being sent back to Argentina, where he would yet again have to admit the collapse of his revolutionary dreams.

Eventually all the Cuban exiles were set free, after apparently paying the habitual *mordida* or bribe to "sort out" their documents. According to Che's Mexican biographer Jorge Castañeda, this was the first time the US intelligence authorities made a note of his "communist" activities, although they seemed to think he was more involved with left-wing Mexican labor leaders than with any revolutionary plans for Cuba.

From now on, there was a rapid countdown to the departure for the island. Fidel Castro was afraid that the group might be picked up again, or be infiltrated by Cuban agents and lose their stockpiles of weapons. They quickly found a secondhand boat belonging to an American, which bizarrely was called *Granma*—after his grandmother. (This unlikely name is the even unlikelier name of the revolutionary Cuban government's state run newspaper, launched in 1965, and a province of the island.) More would-be revolutionaries continued to arrive, perhaps the most important of them being the former tailor and student activist Camilo Cienfuegos, who had been living in exile in the United States and over the next few years was to become another mythical figure in the Cuban revolutionary struggle.

Another hugely important meeting was between Fidel and Frank País, the leader of the July 26 Movement in Santiago, Cuba's second city in the east of the island. Although he advised Fidel to postpone the landing until the urban networks of the movement were better organized—an idea which Fidel rejected—it was he who suggested that if the guerrillas were coming by boat they should aim for an area as close as possible to Santiago, where he and his organization could give them support. There were more meetings with other Cuban opposition groups, but Castro and his followers could not come to an agreement with the communist Partido Socialista Popular (Popular Socialist Party), who wanted a broad opposition front and political action to get rid of Batista rather than a revolutionary war.

In October 1956 Ernesto finally separated from Hilda, who returned with their daughter to Peru. She maintained that their separation was only temporary, forced on them by circumstances, but Ernesto wrote to his old friend Tita Infante that:

> my marriage is almost completely over, and will be completely finished with next month, because then my wife is going to Peru to see her family after an absence of eight years. This break leaves a slightly bitter taste because she was a very loyal companion and her revolutionary conduct during my forced vacation was beyond reproach, but our spiritual discrepancies

were huge, and I always have that anarchic spirit which makes me dream of far horizons…

These horizons were drawing nearer much more rapidly than he might have expected. Fidel discovered another informer in their ranks, and decided that the only thing to do was to leap into the unknown—to set off as quickly as possible. Ernesto wrote in his diary that he and his companions had suddenly got word from Fidel that they should leave Mexico City at the earliest opportunity and meet up on the River Tuxpán in the state of Veracruz on the Gulf of Mexico coast on November 24, 1956. With all his men united around him, Fidel had to choose the eighty one to accompany him on board the *Granma*. In his speech in Revolution Square, Havana, in October 1967 after he had learned of Che's death in Bolivia, Fidel said that the Argentine was second on the list following his brother Raúl. In the early hours of the morning of November 26, 1956 they set sail without lights from the port of Tuxpán, heading out into the Gulf of Mexico, where storms and strong northerly winds had been forecast.

Ernesto "Che" Guevara was aboard, chosen to be the group's doctor in the struggle that awaited them.

3
REVOLUTIONARY WAR
(1956–1959)

C he's medical skills were put to the test almost immediately, though in a far from heroic way. The seas in the Gulf of Mexico were so rough that many of the *Granma*'s occupants were sick for most of the crossing as the leaky, overcrowded launch made its way slowly towards Cuba. In his *Reminiscences of the Cuban Revolutionary War*, Che provides a graphic description of the early stages of the trip:

> With our lights extinguished, we left the port of Tuxpán amid an infernal mess of men and all sorts of material. The weather was very bad and navigation was forbidden, but the river

estuary was calm. We traversed the entrance into the Gulf and a little later turned on our lights. We began a frantic search for the antiseasickness pills, which we did not find. We sang the Cuban national anthem and the "Hymn of the 26th of July" for perhaps five minutes, then the entire boat took on an aspect both ridiculous and tragic: men with anguished faces holding their stomachs, some with their heads in buckets, others lying in the strangest positions, immobile, their clothing soiled with vomit.

To make matters worse, Che had been forced to leave in such a hurry that he had left all his own asthma medicines behind, and so also suffered badly all through the sea journey. To add to the woes of the would-be revolutionaries, a trip that they had planned would take five days stretched out to longer than seven. This delay meant that the uprising led by Frank País and his July 26 Movement supporters in the eastern city of Santiago, which had been timed to coincide with their landing and to help distract Batista's armed forces, had already taken place and been brutally suppressed. It also meant that the reception committee which was to have brought them more weapons and volunteers had given up waiting for them at the appointed spot and left.

The first sight that the Argentine revolutionary had of Cuba early on the morning of December 2, 1956 was not an encouraging one. The *Granma* ran aground on a sandbank more than a mile from the shore at Playa de Las Coloradas, in the southeast of the island near Cape Cruz. The men had to jump from their craft and wade through a tangled mass of mangrove swamps before they could reach dry land. As they were crawling through the trees, the group split up, and it soon became clear that they had been spotted by a coastguard launch, which radioed for aircraft to attack them. In this regard at least they were fortunate, as the dense mangroves made them invisible from the air.

When they regrouped on shore, the sodden group of insurgents met the first peasant farmers of the region, and won some respite, but Fidel Castro quickly gave the order for his men to keep going and head for the highlands of the Sierra Maestra where he wanted to establish their guerrilla camp.

When Fidel Castro, his brother Raúl, Che and the other *Granma* fighters landed in Cuba in December 1956, Fulgencio Batista had been president a second time for more than four years. In fact, he had dominated the Cuban political scene for more than twenty years. Until 1940, as head of the army, he had been content to allow weak civilian leaders to occupy the presidency, while he pulled the strings from the shadows. Then in 1940 he stood for election himself, and was voted in as president of the nation. His first four years in office coincided with a favorable economic situation—like other commodity-exporting countries (including Che's own Argentina) not directly involved in the fighting, the Second World War provided new opportunities for exports.

Cuba's sugar production rose dramatically and profitably as a result. Batista led a social democratic government that secured political support from a broad spectrum of political groups, including the Communist Party. He allowed the party to operate legally, and in return it gave him backing as part of the Soviet Union's anti-Nazi struggle. As a mulatto who stood out against Cuba's white elite, he was also backed by many among the nation's poorer black population, although he did little to advance their cause.

Unlike Argentina and the other countries on the Latin American mainland, Cuba had not gained independence from Spain in the early nineteenth century. Important figures such as José Martí led the fight to overthrow the Spanish in the mid-century, but it was not until 1898 that the Spaniards were dislodged. The forces which defeated them came from the United States, and their victory led to a four-year period of intervention (1898–1902) when Cuba was ruled by an American general. When the US forces withdrew to allow the establishment of the first Cuban Republic, they made sure that the United States continued to be a dominant force in the island's political life. The Platt Amendment gave the United

States the right to intervene in Cuban affairs whenever it judged necessary, and allowed for the establishment of military bases such as Guantánamo. Although the amendment was withdrawn in 1934, a sense of humiliation stemming from the years of occupation and subsequent subservience to US interests fuelled anti-American feeling that Fidel Castro and his revolutionaries quickly turned to their advantage. This feeling would also eventually work against Batista.

At the end of his term in office in 1944, Batista stood down from power, although he retained close links to the armed forces. The next eight years saw leaders from the two main parties—the *Auténticos* of the Authentic Cuban Revolutionary Party and the *Ortodoxos* (the Orthodox Cuban Revolutionary Party)—alternate in power. Under them, corruption increased spectacularly, and the social cohesion that had prevailed under the Batista government soon fell apart. Once more there were stirrings among army officers, and in March 1952 Batista put himself at the head of these discontented military plotters to lead a bloodless coup. He soon had himself named head of state, and this time seemed determined to stay in power indefinitely. During his rule, Cuba became increasingly subordinated to US interests. American firms owned the sugar and other agricultural industries. They ran the services in the cities, and supplied the machinery for everything from the sugar mills to the nickel mines. North American, and often Mafia, interests ran the tourist hotels, casinos and nightclubs that attracted growing numbers of tourists from the United States. Meanwhile, poverty in the countryside worsened, making Cuba one of the most unequal societies in the Americas.

It was not long before political opposition to Batista's rule surfaced. Fidel Castro, who had hoped to stand as an Ortodoxo candidate in the 1952 elections that were forestalled by the Batista coup, was one of many who soon concluded that electoral politics would solve nothing in Cuba.

At dawn on July 26, 1953, Castro and some 120 fighters attacked the Moncada barracks in Santiago. They were hoping to take the garrison by surprise, to seize weapons and to gauge if there was sufficient response from the rest of Cuba to begin a popular insurrection. But little went according to plan: the 400 or more soldiers inside the barracks were quickly alerted to the attack, and fought off the rebels. Fidel and the survivors retreated—it seems that he was still thinking of heading to the mountains and beginning a guerrilla war then and there. The army took vicious reprisals, and as many as 61 men were tortured and killed over the next four days, until the Catholic Church and other civic organizations arranged for the surrender of the remaining rebels without bloodshed. It took another week for the security forces to locate Castro.

The Moncada attack was Castro's attempt to take the lead in fighting the Batista regime, and to show he was determined to confront the dictatorship with force. The aftermath of that failed assault demonstrated what kind of regime Batista ran: after the first bout of indiscriminate killing of those suspects who had been taken prisoner, there were the show trials (in order to keep Washington happy). Castro was allowed to carry out his own defense and managed to turn the occasion into a propaganda coup, following which he was given a lengthy term in jail, only to benefit from an amnesty after two years. This was an old-style Caribbean dictatorship, arbitrary and disorganized, completely dissimilar to the military dictatorships that brought methodical, ideological repression to many countries of Latin America, including Argentina, in the 1970s.

This time Fidel Castro was gambling that by landing and openly defying the dictatorship, he could rally a significant number of Cubans to his side and defeat the Batista regime militarily. The idea of creating a small revolutionary group or *foco* and gradually expanding its influence until it could topple a government owed far more to past struggles in Cuba than to any ideas imported from abroad. In the fight for independence against Spain, as well as in the revolutionary movements of the 1930s, groups of rebels had headed for the hills and tried to attract like-minded supporters to their cause. Castro knew that

Cubans would identify his own move with these earlier uprisings, and thereby lend it authenticity, even though the precise ideological direction of his rebellion was as yet unclear.

Early in December 1957, success for the bedraggled survivors of the *Granma* landing seemed unlikely. Batista had a well-equipped and trained army of at least 15,000 men, more than enough to deal with the motley group of guerrillas who had landed in Oriente province, most of whom had no more military training than the few weeks they had spent practicing shooting and doing physical exercises in Mexico. In fact, Castro and his men were almost wiped out before they could even reach the Sierra Maestra and begin their guerrilla war. Che himself described the disaster which overtook them in the cane-fields of Alegría de Pío only three days after landing. In his version, written up from his daily journal after the guerrillas had triumphed in 1959, this "baptism of fire" was a decisive moment for him. On the run from his attackers, he chose to save a box of ammunition rather than his medical case, thus sealing his determination to be a guerrilla fighter rather than the revolutionaries' doctor.

What happened next is described in detail in *Reminiscences of the Cuban Revolutionary War*:

> I chose the cartridge box, leaving behind the medicine pack, and crossed the clearing which separated me from the cane-field… A burst of gunfire, nothing special about it, hit us. I felt a terrible blow to the chest, and another in the neck, and was sure I was dead…

At that moment, according to his diary, it was a literary memory rather than a revolutionary one that came into his mind:

> I immediately wondered what would be the best way to die, now that all seemed lost. I remembered an old story of Jack London's in which the hero, knowing he is condemned to freeze to death in the icy reaches of Alaska, leans against a tree and decides to end his life with dignity.

The passage is, of course, all the more poignant given the way that Che was to meet his death in the "wastes" of Bolivia scarcely ten years later. This time around, however, he lived to escape from the ambush and to head for the mountains with a small group of men. After more than two weeks' marching at night and staying under cover during the day, Che and his remaining three companions finally met up with Fidel Castro and the twenty or so others who had survived the Alegría de Pío attack.

Fidel Castro had chosen the Sierra Maestra as the launching pad for his revolution for several reasons. It was one of the remotest parts of the island, and contains Cuba's highest mountain: the 2,000-metre Pico Turquino. The peasant farmers scratching a living there were among the most exploited of the island's population. They lived on small holdings from which they were frequently evicted by the big landowners, many of whom only rarely visited the estates they owned, leaving control to overseers whose brutal methods helped predispose many of the peasants to Fidel Castro and his men. Fidel hoped that these poor peasants would not only be sympathetic to his struggle, but would provide him with the new recruits he desperately needed if he was to succeed. At the same time, the Sierra Maestra was also close enough to the eastern cities of Santiago, Manzanillo and Holguín for the organized opposition groups there to be of direct help in supplying the rebels with food and weapons.

After a few weeks in the Sierra Maestra, arms supplied by the July 26 Movement and an influx of new volunteers encouraged Castro to decide that his group was strong enough to go on the offensive. In mid-January 1957, the guerrillas made their first successful assault on a small army post at La Plata, killing several of the soldiers and suffering no losses. In the skirmishes that followed in the days afterwards, Che was involved in close combat with more government soldiers. As Jon Lee Anderson writes:

> Che recovered the rifle and cartridge belt of the soldier he
> had hit, then inspected the body. "He had a bullet under the

heart with exit on the right side. He was dead." To his certain knowledge, Che had killed his first man.

Soon afterwards, the leaders of the July 26 Movement came up to the sierra to coordinate the campaign against Batista with Fidel. To the guerrilla leader, the fact that they came to him proved that he was in the ascendancy. Over several days of talk he managed to convince them that the movement should swing all its weight behind his efforts in the mountains, rather than opening another front elsewhere, or leading the revolutionary effort from the cities. Che, who was not part of the inner circle at this time, seems to have dismissed the leaders from the *llano* (the plains) as middle-class intellectuals with "anti-communist inclinations," although he was impressed by the young Frank País, the head of the movement in the city of Santiago.

Fidel also scored another propaganda coup in these early months; although the Batista regime regularly proclaimed that the rebels had already been wiped out, and that Castro himself had been killed, the rebel leader gave an interview in his Sierra Maestra camp to the veteran *New York Times* reporter Herbert Matthews. In a series of articles published back in the United States, Matthews wrote of Fidel Castro:

> It is easy to see why he has caught the imagination of the youth of Cuba all over the island. Here was an educated, dedicated fanatic, a man of ideals, of courage, and of remarkable qualities of leadership.

The American journalist concluded even then that

> from the look of things, General Batista cannot possibly hope to suppress the Castro revolt.

At this time, Che was still officially the insurgent group's doctor. In his diary he wrote of the "complex I had about being a foreigner," and he was also finding it extremely hard to adapt to the harsh conditions of life in the heavily-forested, treacherous terrain of the Sierra Maestra. He contracted malaria, and suffered from more bad attacks of asthma, which slowed him up and made

Fidel Castro (left) and Che Guevara, Sierra Maestra, 1957

it painful for him to march as quickly as the others. As usual, he overcame the difficulties by sheer strength of will. He also saw the importance of winning over the local population, and gave medical consultations to anybody who wanted them. For many, this was the first time in their lives that they had ever received medical attention of any sort. As a doctor, he was unable to offer them very much, because most of the peasants' illnesses were due to the harsh conditions and lack of nourishment that were their daily reality, but what he saw only served to strengthen his political convictions:

we began to appreciate in our own flesh and blood the need for a definitive change in the life of the people. The idea of agrarian reform became clear, and oneness with the people ceased being theory and was converted into a fundamental part of our being.

Quite quickly, though, Che's position in the rebel army changed. Following another attack on an army post, he was given the task of bringing the wounded men safely out of the area and back to the guerrilla base camp in the safety of the Sierra Maestra. His success in this difficult operation, as well as the growing respect he won from the others in the insurgent army, led Fidel Castro to give him greater responsibilities as a military leader. On July 17, 1957, shortly after Che's thirtieth birthday, he was promoted to the rank of "captain" and put at the head of a column of 75 men. Soon after this, he was awarded the rank of *comandante*—the highest military position in the rebel group. With the rank came the black beret and the tin star that over the next few years were to become an essential part of the "Che" legend.

By now, six months after the guerrillas' incursion into Cuban territory, the fighting against Batista's forces was becoming increasingly bitter. The army took vicious reprisals against the local peasants to prevent them aiding the rebels. Some of the new recruits to the insurgent band could not stand the hardships and discipline of the rebel camp, and tried to desert. There was also a huge problem of informers or *chivatos*, who gave away the rebels' position and movements, while others took advantage of the chaotic situation to resort to banditry in the hills, terrorizing the population for their own gain. In this confused situation, Che's moral rectitude again made him stand out from the others. He was unbendingly intolerant of deserters and infiltrators, and usually demanded they be shot after only the most summary of trials. His uncompromising attitude has led even a generally sympathetic biographer such as Jon Lee Anderson to conclude: "Che's trail through the Sierra Maestra was littered with the bodies of *chivatos*, deserters, and delinquents, men whose deaths *he* had ordered and in some cases carried out himself."

Che's critics see this as an early example of his extremism and inhuman attitude towards others, which they regard to as confirmed by the way he acted when appointed to judge collaborators of the Batista regime in Havana after the triumph of the uprising. Che himself explained the executions carried out in the sierra in his *Reminiscences of the Cuban Revolutionary War*:

> that moment called for an iron fist. We were obliged to inflict exemplary punishment in order to curb violations of discipline and to liquidate the nuclei of anarchy which sprang up in areas lacking a stable government.

In October 1957, still less than a year after the *Granma* expedition had disembarked so uncertainly, Che was put in charge of a permanent camp in the Sierra Maestra. This was El Hombrito, and from the start he was determined that it should be an example of the kind of society that he, Fidel Castro and the others were fighting for. The camp was based on productive activities: a bakery was set up, a workshop for making rudimentary weapons, another for shoes and other leather goods—there was even—this being Cuba—a rudimentary cigar production facility. In addition, Che set about spreading the news of what the rebels had achieved and how they saw the world; he began to produce and regularly write for a mimeographed newsletter called *El cubano libre* (*The Free Cuban*). At the same time, he set up classes to teach the young recruits in the rebel army how to read and write, as well as giving them political instruction. According to his own later account, they and the local peasants quickly and willingly accepted socialism, and this experience undoubtedly helped confirm him in his ideas of what a post-revolutionary society should be like.

This period of relative stability and calm did not last long. At the end of November 1957, Captain Sánchez Mosquera, whom Che described as "one of the most tenacious, aggressive and bloody enemy officers," led his troops up a valley close to the camp and eventually succeeded in overrunning it. In the fighting, Che was wounded again, this time in the foot. Luckily, by now he was not the only doctor around: one of the new recruits, a medical student, cut out the bullet with a razor blade. Although Che and his men had been forced to retreat, they had depleted Batista's forces to the extent that they did not pursue them higher into the mountains, preferring to withdraw altogether. This gave the rebels the chance to regroup, and to set up another base camp at La Mesa, where Che patiently set about rebuilding the infrastructure he had put in place in the previous camp.

By the start of 1958, therefore, there was a state of "armed truce" in the Sierra Maestra. The rebel army had consolidated its position, and its numbers were slowly growing. Batista's army harassed them, using planes to bomb what were thought to be their positions, but did not send troops into the immediate area. By February 1958 Che was sufficiently confident of the outcome of the revolutionary struggle to set up a radio station, Radio Rebelde, which claimed to be broadcasting from the "free territory of Cuba," even though at first its only verified listener was a single peasant farmer living across the valley from their camp.

Soon, however, the radio was transferred to Fidel Castro's column, and according to Che at least, "by December 1958 [it] had become one of the Cuban radio stations with the highest rating." Although much of Che's achievements in the mountains have an air of improvisation about them, they followed a simple but definite strategy, also outlined in *Reminiscences of the Cuban Revolutionary War*:

> The guerrillero's problems were very simple: to subsist as an individual, he needed small amounts of food, certain indispensable items of clothing and medicaments; to subsist as a guerrilla force, that is an armed force in struggle, he needed arms and ammunition; for his political development he needed channels of propaganda. In order to assure these minimal necessities, a communications and information apparatus was required.

Now that their situation on the ground had stabilized, it was the political direction of the fight against Batista which became more urgent. Fidel Castro was anxious not to be isolated from the activists of the July 26 Movement in the towns and cities of Oriente province—principally Santiago and Manzanillo. He also wanted to exert influence in the center of power on the island, the capital Havana. Already in July 1957 he had issued a "Manifesto of the Sierra Maestra," published together with members of the nonviolent political opposition to Batista. Che, for his part, saw these leaders as "bourgeois opportunists," but also admitted that the pact was probably necessary at the time—although it could be broken if and when the military campaign against Batista proved successful. In December 1957 the leading figures of the other opposition groups came up with what was known as the "Miami Pact," in which they sought to define how power would be distributed after the fall of the dictator. When news of this pact filtered back to the Sierra Maestra, Che was horrified: it seemed to him to seek simply to remove Batista from power and then continue as before. There was no mention in the pact of agrarian reform, no proposed changes to the economic system, and worst of all, it stipulated that the guerrilla forces should be amalgamated into the national army, which would not even be cleansed of its Batista-supporting elements. Che urged Castro to reject the pact, and a few days later was gratified when Fidel condemned it totally, reaffirming that:

> The leadership of the struggle against the tyranny is and will continue to be in Cuba and in the hands of the revolutionary fighters.

Fidel Castro's position with regard to two other anti-Batista groups still had to be properly defined. The first of these was the July 26 Movement. He saw himself as the movement's "natural" leader: it was he, after all, who had led the attack on the Moncada barracks in 1953, which had marked the beginning of the armed campaign against Batista. He was now leading his "revolutionary fighters" in direct confrontation with the dictator's army. He expected the movement's directorate in the cities to recognize his position and to follow his commands rather than pursue a strategy of their own. When an attempted general strike and insurrection in April 1958 organized by the movement was an almost complete failure, Castro was quick to distance himself from its other main leaders. Instead, he sought an alliance with the Popular Socialist Party (the name adopted by the Cuban Communist Party), which until then had been wary of joining in what it saw as his military "adventurism." He also decided that in order to show he really was in command of the fight against Batista, he would take the fight out of the Sierra Maestra and spread it into as much of the island as possible.

Che himself had always been critical of the July 26 Movement. In his essay *One Year of Armed Struggle*, written after the revolutionary victory, he explains why he considered insurrectionary force more valuable than the opposition in the cities:

> The July 26 Movement, participating as an unarmed ally, could not have changed the picture, even if its leaders had seen the outcome clearly, which they did not. The lesson for the future is: he who has the strength dictates the strategy.

After the failure of the April 1958 call for action, he bitterly criticized the organizers for "sectarianism" (because they had not included the communists in their plans), for military incompetence in trying to organize a militia without proper selection or training, and for exposing the civilian population to reprisals. His conclusion was this:

> the large-scale killing of civilians, repeated failures, murders committed by the dictatorship in various aspects of the struggle we have analyzed, point to guerrilla action on favorable terrain as the best expression of the technique of popular struggle against a despotic and still-strong government.

The Batista regime had already qualified Guevara as a "foreign communist." In a March 1958 interview with the Argentine journalist Jorge Ricardo Masetti, who had found his way up to the Sierra Maestra mountains, Che admitted as much, although it did not seem to bother him. He described Fidel Castro as

> an extraordinary man [who] had an exceptional faith in that once he left for Cuba, he would arrive. And that once he arrived, he would fight. And that fighting, he would win. I shared his optimism.

Whatever his own political persuasion, he said, the revolution they were attempting to create was "revolutionary nationalist" in character. He also told Masetti that he considered his "fatherland" to be not merely Argentina but the whole of the Americas, and contrasted his presence in Cuba with the constant interference of the United States in the country's affairs, which went unchallenged. Masetti returned to Argen-tina with his scoop, little imagining then how his and Che's paths were to cross again in the future.

The emerging revolutionary hero had kept only sporadic links with his family in Argentina. He wrote occasionally to his mother and to other relatives, but above all his personal life seemed to have been relegated to a distant corner of his memory, as he made himself into a revolutionary commander entirely at the service of the cause.

Another person to suffer from this distancing was his wife, Hilda Gadea. Back in Lima, she became the July 26 Movement's representative in Peru, and helped raised money, spread its message and receive Cuban exiles. But when she wrote to Che asking if she and the two-year-old Hildita could come to the Cuban mountains to share in the struggle, she eventually received the dusty reply that the time was not ripe for her to come, as the rebels were planning an offensive and Guevara had no idea where he might be from one day to the next.

This was true, but only in part. Another reason for his reluctance to have Hilda join him may have been the fact that for the first time since the *Granma* fighters had arrived in the mountains, Che was seen regularly with a woman. This was

Zoila Rodríguez, an eighteen-year-old mulata with a child. The two met when she helped shoe Che's mule. As she recalled years afterwards:

> As I was shoeing the mule, I looked at him out of the corner of my eye. I realized he was observing me, but he was looking at me in the way boys look at girls, and I got really nervous.

She soon overcame her nerves, and for several months afterwards they shared life in the rebel camp at Minas del Frío, until she was replaced by another companion who was to prove even more important in the life of the comandante.

As Che wrote, in the early months of 1958 the Batista government was still strong, especially after the failure of the call for a general uprising against it. May 1958 saw a big army push into the sierra. Its leader, General Cantillo, had some 10,000 troops at his command, although a third of them were new recruits, drafted in to face the rebel insurgents, and were neither trained nor used to combat. The plan was to encircle Fidel Castro's forces in the mountains; it was a realistic aim, for despite Castro's grandiloquent talk of a rebel army acting on several fronts, he could still count on only some 300 men, many of them also untested in battle, and controlling very little territory.

At first, the army offensive was successful. Thanks to air bombardments as well as sheer numbers, they pressed the rebel forces hard. Che was called on to bolster the lines of defense, and to help quickly train the new recruits so that they could be brought up into the firing line. Despite their early successes, the regular army forces did not know the terrain as well as Fidel and Che's men, who were able to withdraw from combat and then ambush the advancing troops, as well as encircle their camps.

During these crucial weeks, Che was virtually Fidel's second-in-command, since Castro's brother Raúl had opened a second front further east in Oriente province, and Camilo Cienfuegos was outside the Sierra Maestra with another column of fighters. Now Che proved that he had learned his lesson over the previous year, and in his military operations mixed daring with caution. He was beginning to believe that not only would

Raúl Castro, left, and Che during the final push against the Batista regime

the revolutionaries win, but that he himself would survive to play a role beyond that of a guerrilla leader.

Gradually the tide turned in favor of the rebels. Fidel laid siege to an army camp at Jigüe, and forced its surrender on July 20. Che did the same at the Las Vegas army encampment. By August 1958 Batista's troops had pulled out of the Sierra Maestra entirely. The military offensive had failed, and in the Oriente the government forces were on the verge of collapse. Some of the officers and soldiers even changed sides and joined the rebel forces, calculating that their future prospects were better with them.

Fidel was anxious to press home his advantage, and to prove that the rebellion was nationwide in scope, rather than confined to one mountainous region. Che was ordered to train more new arrivals and to lead a column off to Las Villas province in the center of the island. Using the Escambray mountains as his base, his task was to ensure that the main highway and other communication routes between Havana and the east were cut off. Camilo was sent with a smaller column of men to travel even further west, to Pinar del Río. Fidel himself was to move out from the mountains to the eastern plains, where he would join his brother Raúl in the push on Santiago and other towns in Oriente.

Throughout the second half of August 1958, Che was busy recruiting volunteers and organizing their departure, but just as they were about to pull out, Batista's troops captured the column's vehicles, and with them all the gas Che had been storing for use in his jeeps. This reverse meant that he had to set off on foot with 148 men on a march of more than 350 miles. As he recalled in *Reminiscences of the Cuban Revolutionary War*:

> We had to cross rivers in flood, creeks and brooks converted into rivers; we had to struggle unendingly to keep ammunition, guns, and rockets dry; we had to find fresh horses to replace the tired ones; we had increasingly to avoid populated areas as we moved beyond Oriente province. We marched toilsomely through flooded terrain, attacked by hordes of mosquitoes which made rest stops unbearable.

To make things worse, they soon came into contact with government troops, who harried them continuously. Even so, by October 16 Che and his men had successfully reached the mountains of Las Villas. Their immediate task was to ensure that the presidential elections of November 1958, after which Batista was offering to step down in favour of a hand-picked civilian, should not be seen as the legitimate expression of the Cuban people's wishes. To achieve this aim the guerrillas blocked roads and harangued meetings of peasants, and succeeded in reducing participation in what Guevara called the "electoral farce" to a minimum.

At the same time, Che found that he had to assert his authority over several other groups that had risen up against the Batista regime in the region, as well as enlisting the wholehearted support of the July 26 Movement in the local towns and cities, especially the regional center of Santa Clara. This city of 150,000 people was the fourth largest in Cuba and was a prime target for the rebel force, as it held the key to communications between Havana and the east of the island. Che took his usual hard line with all possible competing groups, insisting that they join him and recognize his fighters as the military and moral leaders of the struggle. Even the notoriously individualistic Eloy Gutiérrez Menoyo, who had been operating with his own small guerrilla force in the Escambray mountains since early 1957, came to accept his authority.

As in the Sierra Maestra, Che quickly set up a base camp and turned it into a thriving productive center. Cabellete de Casas became a military training school for new recruits; there were facilities to produce a newsletter, *El Miliciano*, as well as the usual attempts to make the camp self-reliant with food. It was here also that Guevara first began consciously to gather men around him whom he could trust to help him in whatever role he was assigned after the rebel victory, which seemed to him increasingly certain. Yet it was the presence of a woman in Cabellete de Casas that was perhaps most significant. This was Aleida March, a twenty-four-year-old teacher. She was the link between the group in the mountains and the July 26 Movement in Santa Clara; after her house was raided in November 1958 it was unsafe for her to go back to the city, and so she transferred to the guerrilla camp. In her recently published *Evocation*, the woman who was to become the *comandante*'s second wife recalls her first meeting with him in these terms:

> Marta [Lugioyo] asked me what I thought of him. I replied without hesitation that he wasn't bad looking, and that the most interesting thing about him was his look, or rather his way of looking. I thought of him as an older man. Marta said she thought he had beautiful hands—something which I did not

notice at the time, but which I was able to confirm later on.

Aleida's arrival coincided with an army offensive designed to drive Che out of the mountains. After six days' fighting at the beginning of December 1958, he and his forces succeeded not only in pushing the troops back, but in going on the offensive themselves, severing vital road links, destroying bridges and isolating the army in town garrisons.

It was not long before Aleida and Che became inseparable. As she tells the story, one night during the guerrillas' offensive push, she found it impossible to sleep. As she was sitting by the roadside in the early morning, Che pulled up in a jeep. "I'm going to attack Cabaiguán," he said, "want to come along?" "Sure," she replied, "and from that moment on I never left his side—or let him out of my sight."

On December 16, his guerrillas blew up the main road and rail bridges near Santa Clara, cutting the city off from the east of the country, where Raúl Castro was steadily advancing towards Santiago. The last fortnight of 1958 saw Che and his men taking all the towns around Santa Clara. In less than two weeks, Che took over territory where more than a quarter of a million people lived. His men had overrun twelve army and police posts, taking more than 800 prisoners. Only eleven members of the guerrilla forces had been killed. But both sides knew that the battle for the city was to be the crucial moment of his campaign. Batista had ordered reinforcements to be sent there, so that as Che laid his plans for attack, there were some 3,500 government troops with heavy weapons and backed by the airforce, ready to defend their positions. Against them, Che had only 350 men.

The rebels began their push on the city on December 29, 1958. One of their chief targets was an armored train loaded with weapons, ammunition and communications equipment that had been sent to bolster the city's defenses. To prevent its escape, Che ordered his men to bulldoze the railway tracks leading out of the city. When the soldiers on board the convoy tried to break out of the guerrilla encirclement, the armored railway engine and several of the carriages were derailed.

Che describes the battle that ensued:

the men in the armored train had been dislodged by our Molotov cocktails; in spite of their excellent protection they were prepared to fight only at long range, from comfortable positions, and against a virtually disarmed enemy—in the true style of colonizers versus the Indians of the North American West. Harassed by our men who, from nearby train carriages and other close-range positions, were hurling bottle of flaming gasoline, the train— thanks to its armor-plate— became a veritable oven for its soldiers. After several hours, the entire crew surrendered, with their twenty-two armored cars, their anti-aircraft guns, their DCA machine guns, their fabulous quantities of ammunition (fabulous, that is, to us).

This became one of the most famous episodes in the entire guerrilla war. It is commemorated in the propaganda film made by the revolutionary ICAIC film production company, and features prominently in the Museum of the Revolution in Santa Clara. As the guerrillas pushed on towards the center of the city, many of its inhabitants also joined in the battle against the army and the police. Slowly over the next three days the forces loyal to Batista were surrounded and overwhelmed.

In Havana, meanwhile, Batista had realized he was lost. At a New Year's Eve party, he called his generals together and told them he was resigning the presidency and handing over power to the head of the armed forces, General Eulogio Cantillo. In the early hours of January 1, 1959, he boarded a plane with forty members of his family and closest collaborators and flew to the Dominican Republic, where his fellow dictator Rafael Trujillo was happy to receive him. Batista later moved to Estoril in Portugal, where he was chairman of a Spanish-owned life insurance company until his death in 1973.

When the news of Batista's flight reached Santa Clara, the garrison of more than one thousand soldiers still holding out against the rebels finally surrendered. This was Che Guevara's greatest military victory, won in no small measure thanks to his own personal inspiration as leader and tactician.

Fidel Castro (being embraced) arrives in Havana. Che Guevara is seated at his left. January 8, 1959.

In 1997, thirty years after his death, the city was chosen as the final resting place for his remains after they were returned to Cuba from Bolivia. Santa Clara also houses a museum devoted to telling the story of his life, and a reconstruction of the famous battle over the armored train.

As the new year of 1959 dawned, Che knew that this was no time to rest on his laurels. "We've won the war, now we have to start the revolution," he told a colleague. As soon as he communicated news of the Santa Clara victory to Fidel Castro in the east of the island, he was told to prepare for the push on Havana. Castro was determined that it should be his troops and his July 26 Movement which should take all the credit for ousting the dictator. He wanted his most trusted lieutenants in place with their troops to make it clear who was in charge. So Camilo Cienfuegos led his rebel column towards the capital, followed by Comandante Che Guevara.

4
THE REVOLUTION IN POWER
(1959–1965)

On January 2, 1959, Fidel Castro proclaimed the victory of the revolution in Santiago de Cuba, which had fallen to rebel forces commanded by him and his brother Raúl. He instructed the two revolutionary *comandantes*, Camilo Cienfuegos and Ernesto "Che" Guevara, to travel to Havana before him, to make sure that there was no power vacuum after the fall of Batista. As befitted a Cuban, Cienfuegos was given the honor of being the first guerrilla leader to enter the city. He and his men took over Camp Colombia, the main army barracks in the center of Havana, which they renamed "Camp Libertad," while Che and his "Ciro Redondo" column headed for the La Cabaña fortress, the eighteenth-century Spanish castle that dominates the harbour area. Che arrived in the early hours of January 3, 1959. This was his first view of the capital of a country of some six million inhabitants on whose behalf he had been fighting in rugged mountains for more than two years.

As usual, Che traveled in his jeep wearing what was by now the symbolic trademark of his rebel uniform—the black beret with the red star of revolution on it. In the vehicle with him were his trusted bodyguards and one other very important passenger: Aleida March. According to her recent memoirs, it was during this drive on the capital that Che "made his first declaration of love." For her and most of the other insurgents, it was also the first time they had set sight on the Cuban capital; they had spent all their lives in the east of the island, and had never ventured to the big city before. Aleida recalls that their driver pulled up at a red light, thinking it was a traffic signal, until he finally realized it was a pharmacy shop sign. When Che and his column eventually reached the fortress, the 3,000 regular troops stationed there accepted his command without a word of protest or regret. Che's first words in charge were dismissive: he told the assembled troops that they could probably teach his men to drill, but that the guerrillas would teach them how to fight.

After a few days, Che flew to meet Fidel Castro in the east. This was the first time the two men had met since the Argentine had led his column out of the Sierra Maestra some six months earlier. Castro was in no great hurry to reach Havana: he wanted the sense of expectation and curiosity to build up as much as possible. His triumphal entry took place on January 8, by which time the city had been secured and there was a tremendous sense of jubilation. Castro, dressed as usual in military fatigues, was careful to address the vast crowds in reassuring terms. He promised to include everyone in the new, post-Batista Cuba, but otherwise said little specific about the political aims of the revolution. He did, however, make good his commitment to appoint the independent judge Manuel Urrutia as the new president, while he himself became commander-in-chief of what were renamed the Rebel Armed Forces. Even the United States seemed satisfied that the new government was legitimate, and was quick to recognize it.

Yet despite of these attempts to reach out to the different forces which had opposed the dictator, there was an immediate, intense struggle to shape the future political direction of the country. Most of the decisions were taken in the villa that Fidel Castro took over in Cojimar, the old fishing port east of the capital that Ernest Hemingway had made famous in his 1952 novel, *The Old Man and the Sea*. It was here that the revolutionaries discussed not only the details of the proposed agrarian reform and the country's new constitution, but held meetings with representatives of the Communist (Popular Socialist) Party in order to cement their support.

Che and Fidel's younger brother Raúl Castro were those closest to the communists. They had both already demonstrated their attraction to Marxism while fighting in the mountains, despite the initial reluctance of the party to support what according to communist orthodoxy was seen as "military adventurism"—because the fight was led by a guerrilla band rather than organized labor. In typical fashion, Che was quick to publicly define what he saw as the tasks of the revolutionaries in power. Speaking at the Sociedad Cultural Nuestro Tiempo in late January 1959 on the "social projections of the rebel army," he insisted that their fight had not ended with military victory over the Batista forces. It was the revolutionary army's duty, he said, to ensure that Cuban society was totally changed. This process would start with a thorough-going agrarian reform in which land would be taken over by the state. The next step would be an accelerated process of industrialization, so that Cuba would no longer be dependent on importing capital goods—machinery and so on—from abroad. This process of building up industry and self-reliance could not be achieved,

Che argued, without the complete nationalization of the means of production.

As if this radical vision was not enough to alarm the non-communists in Cuba and foreign observers in Washington and elsewhere, he made it clear that he saw the guerrillas' success on the island as merely the first step towards revolution throughout Latin America, based on rural insurgency and direct military confrontation with those in power. By now, he was in charge of training the new rebel army at La Cabaña, and was appointed head of its military intelligence services. As part of this military infrastructure, he soon set up a "liberation department" to create and strengthen links with left-wing guerrilla groups throughout the Caribbean and Latin America.

But it was yet another of Che's functions in the early days of the revolutionary regime that has proved most contentious. He was put in overall charge of the trials being held against hundreds of leading figures and lesser collaborators in the Batista regime. These trials were held in the evenings, and were usually over and done with in a few hours; those found guilty of torture and other crimes were taken out and summarily shot. Che was not directly involved in the legal processes, but did sign many of the death sentences, which in the first few months of 1959 involved several hundred people. Some of the trials were eventually held in sports stadiums and televised, but this caused such a strong reaction, particularly in the United States, that in the end it was Fidel Castro himself who called a halt to them. As he had shown when dealing with possible informers and traitors in the Sierra Maestra, Che Guevara was convinced that revolutionary justice had to strike hard at its enemies in order to prevent the injustices they represented ever happening again, and so signed many death sentences without any apparent qualms.

It was also in these first weeks of the revolution that Guevara officially became a Cuban. In the new constitution, promulgated on February 9, 1959, anyone who had fought against Batista for more than two years and had been a *comandante* of the rebel forces for a year or more, was declared a Cuban citizen from birth. This honorary citizenship was extremely important to Che, although during his years in Cuba his abruptness and self-confidence—characteristics seen by many as typically "Argentine"—seem hardly to have been modified in any way.

Meanwhile, events in Che's personal life seemed to be evolving at the same vertiginous speed as his public roles. First his parents came to visit and stayed a month, during which time his deep regard for his mother and his difficult relationship with his father quickly became obvious for everyone to see. Soon afterwards, his wife Hilda and daughter Hildita finally came to join him from Peru. He immediately told Hilda he had a new companion, and within a few weeks his Peruvian comrade had agreed not only to a divorce, but to staying on in Cuba with her daughter. Che was married to Aleida March in a civil ceremony on June 2, 1959. He wore his customary military fatigues: she wore white.

The marriage was a hurried affair because Fidel Castro, who by this time was prime minister and held most of the real power in Cuba, had decided to send Che off on an extended trip abroad. He was anxious to present the new face of Cuba to allies in the Third World, to explore new markets for Cuba's sugar crop if the United States reneged on its deals to take most of the annual harvest, and to attract new investment and aid. It also seems possible that Fidel wanted his Argentine lieutenant, who was increasingly making it clear that he saw the revolution in the making as a socialist one, out of the country while he juggled his political alliances and attempted to avoid a complete break with the United States. Over the next three months, Che and his small retinue visited fourteen countries, from Japan to Yugoslavia, India to Egypt. The revolutionary leader showed his usual disdain for protocol and rhetoric, but at the same time demonstrated great interest in any new project aimed at increasing national self-sufficiency, while skilfully negotiating possible deals for sugar or machinery.

As ever, it was only in his correspondence with his relatives back in Buenos Aires that he allowed the more human side of his nature to show through. In a letter to his mother, he recalled ambitions that were after all only a few years old:

> My old dream to visit all these countries takes place now in a way that inhibits all my happiness. I speak of political and economic problems, give parties where the only thing missing is for me to wear a tuxedo, and have to put aside my purest pleasures, which would be to go and dream in the shade of a pyramid or over Tutankhamen's sarcophagus...I am still the same loner I always was, looking for my path without personal help, but now I possess the sense of my historic duty. I have no home, no wife, no children, nor parents, brothers, or sisters, my friends are my friends as long as they think politically like I do, and yet I am content.

Back in Cuba in September 1959, this sense of historic duty led him to take on new responsibilities. A first agrarian reform act had been passed; the largest properties were expropriated and turned into state-run cooperatives. A national institute for agrarian reform (INRA) had been set up. What Fidel Castro now asked Che to do was to head the "industrialization" program allied to these reforms: to study how to make not only Cuban agriculture but its other industries less reliant on foreign inputs of capital, machinery and planning. In 1959 this nationalized industrial sector was a disparate collection of small factories and workshops that Che and his associates had to organize, plan, and make productive. At first, Che was concerned above all that these firms should continue to employ as many people as before: the last thing he and the revolution needed was to add to the half a million or more unemployed who already existed in Cuba. While he was busy trying to get to grips with his new tasks—and learning the mathematics needed to help him in economic planning—he suffered a grievous personal blow. Camilo Cienfuegos, his closest friend and ally from the days of the sierra, was killed in an air accident that has never been properly explained. As well as their devotion to the revolution, the two men shared a disregard for danger and a great sense of humor; Camilo was the person who for Che represented all that was best about the Cuban spirit. Che turned a tribute to his lost friend into a bitter and defiant assessment of the pressures the Cuban revolutionaries were feeling by the end of October 1959:

> The enemy killed him, because it wanted his death. It killed him because we have no safe aircraft, because our pilots cannot get the necessary experience, because, overwhelmed with work as he was, he wanted to be in Havana in as few hours as possible... his own character also killed him. Camilo never measured danger, he turned it into a hobby, he played with it, fought with it as though it were a bull, taunting it, manipulating it; to his guerrilla mentality, no storm cloud should ever be allowed to hold him back or make him change course.

A further homage came soon afterwards with the publication of his book *Guerrilla Warfare*, dedicated to his fallen comrade. Drawing conclusions from his and Camilo's experiences in the sierra, Che here stresses that "popular forces can win a war against an army." The book is also a continuation of his attack on the official Communist Party line (as promoted from Moscow) that the "conditions" for a revolutionary take-over were not present in Cuba : "we do not have to wait for the proper conditions to present themselves, an insurrectionary *foco* can create them," Che insisted. He also emphasised his belief, which again ran counter to the orthodox communist line, that the revolution in Latin America must come from the countryside rather than through organized labor in the towns and cities. An even more personal tribute to Cienfuegos followed on May 20, 1962. It was then that Che's first son was born, to be named Camilo.

As well as *Guerrilla Warfare*, Che published *Reminiscences of the Guerrilla War*, based on notes he had made during the campaigns in the Sierra Maestra and Las Villas province. Once again, his capacity as a writer of bold narrative, in which closely-observed details form part of a lucidly presented overall picture together with a sense of honesty about his descriptions of situations and emotions, contributes to lifting the book out of the ordinary. At the same time, Che pursued his interest in having the revolutionary government's version of events in Cuba and the rest of the world reach a wider audience. With the help of his Argentine colleague Jorge Ricardo Masetti, he set up the Prensa Latina news agency. This was designed to try to break the monopoly on news enjoyed by the big US and European agencies such as Associated Press, UPI or Reuters. Over the next few years, Prensa Latina developed its own strong sense of identity, and attracted contributors of the calibre of Gabriel García Márquez and many other left-wing Latin American writers. But Che's involvement with Masetti went far beyond setting up the news agency. In meeting Masetti again, Che was also interested in the possibility of spreading the Cuban revolution specifically to his home country. According to Fidel Castro, from the very start of the guerrilla adventure back in Mexico, Che had asked him to promise he would be free some day to "make a revolution in Argentina." Fidel had agreed, and in return Che had pledged to devote himself for some years to Cuba.

That devotion to the revolutionary cause in his adopted homeland soon took a surprising turn. On November 26, 1959 Che found himself chairman of Cuba's National Bank. The way that he was appointed to the post has passed into legend. According to Alfredo Guevara, one of Fidel's closest associates who had been with him since his student days, the leaders of the revolution would often meet in the Cojimar villa to discuss future plans until late into the night. It was not unusual for Castro to come and join them, and on one such occasion he apparently burst in and asked, "who's a good economist here?" When Che was the first to reply, he immediately said: "Fine, as from tomorrow you can be head of the National Bank," and left. When Alfredo Guevara and the others expressed their surprise, Che looked sheepish and said: "Economist? I thought Fidel said "who's a good communist?"" Although undoubtedly apocryphal, this anecdote does suggest to what extent the new leaders of Cuba were improvising as they went along, as well as Che's willingness to take on any challenge.

Che's time in charge of the National Bank is remembered above all for his cavalier signing of new banknotes with his nickname "Che" scrawled almost insolently across the back of them. Whether this was intentional disregard for paper money or not, during his time as head of the bank he was already thinking about the value of money in a planned, increasingly socialist economy. This debate was to surface a few years later in 1963-64, but in November 1959 the Argentine who was signing Cuba's new banknotes was more concerned to learn the rudiments of banking, how to control capital flight, inflationary pressures, and what to do with the private banks inherited from the Batista era, many of them run from the United States. For once, his father's quip when he heard the news of the appointment seems reasonable: "My son Ernesto in charge of the funds of the Cuban Republic? Fidel must be mad. Every time a Guevara starts a business, it goes bust."

By 1960 the confrontation with the United States was becoming more dramatic by the day. In January the Cuban government took over all large cattle ranches and sugar plantations, including American-owned ones, a move which prompted letters of protest from the Eisenhower admini-stration. As relations with Washington became ever frostier, Fidel Castro turned increasingly towards the Soviet Union. Deputy Prime Minister Anastas Mikoyan visited Cuba, and both trade and arms deals were signed. The increasing political polarization on the island was meanwhile reflected by numerous acts of sabotage, which the Cuban authorities blamed on US sponsorship. One of these involved an explosion on board the French freighter *La Coubre* in Havana harbor on March 4, 1960 as munitions from Belgium were being unloaded. At least 75 people were killed in what the Cuban government alleged was a CIA-inspired plot, and more than 200 wounded.

According to one version of events, Che was at work at the nearby INRA office when he heard the enormous blast.

Rushing in a car to the scene of the explosion, he assisted wounded victims among the dock workers and crew members. A second explosion rocked the dockside area but Che was unharmed.

At the funeral for some of the victims the following day, the photographer Alberto Díaz, nicknamed "Korda," was struck by the look of restrained fury on Che's face among the funeral cortege. He immediately took two photographs of him, with his long hair sticking out of the inevitable black beret and wearing a tight leather jacket. A few years later, the Italian publisher Giacomo Feltrinelli saw the photo and made a poster of it. Over the years, this has become *the* iconic image of Che, found on millions of students' bedroom walls and even more T-shirts, and used to promote any number of products in the capitalist world. It was only towards the end of his life that Alberto Korda (who claimed he never made any money out of one of the world's most reproduced photos) decided to sue a company for using it to promote their product. The case was against the vodka distillers Smirnoff, who in 2001 wanted to use Che's image in a publicity campaign in the United Kingdom. Korda's authorship of the image was finally recognized, and he was awarded £50,000 in damages—which he donated to the Cuban health system.

It is in this image that Che most looks like an Old Testament prophet, gazing into the distance with a desire for retribution and justice etched on his stern features.

Over the next few months, polarization and tensions within Cuba continued. The government took over several national newspapers, and found itself confronting the powerful Catholic Church, which was increasingly concerned about the direction in which the revolution was heading, especially when in May 1960 Cuba re-established diplomatic relations with Moscow (broken off in the 1950s). It was Che himself, in his capacity as chairman of the National Bank, who was responsible for the next downturn in relations with Washington. Three foreign oil companies owned the major refinery facilities on the island.

The new government owed them more than 50 million dollars in back payments for gasoline it had ordered. Che Guevara then told the companies in no uncertain terms that in order to recoup the debt, they would have to agree to buy and process some 300,000 barrels of the Soviet oil he had arranged to buy. When they refused, the government simply took them over and nationalized them. This move was soon followed by the takeover of foreign-owned utility services.

In response, the Eisenhower administration in Washington immediately cut its Cuban sugar quota. For years, the United States had bought almost all Cuba's sugar output at higher than international market prices, mostly as a gesture of political support to right-wing and military governments. Che had already denounced this arrangement as implying "economic slavery" for the Cuban people, since it tied them into a monoculture economy and did not allow them to diversify agricultural production. But at the same time, it provided guaranteed revenue for the Cuban government, and to lose it after months of threats from Washington promised to be a severe blow. Castro retaliated by bringing in legislation allowing the nationalization of all US-owned properties on the island, while the Soviet Union stepped in to announce it would buy the entire surplus sugar crop of 700,000 tons. Cuba was rapidly becoming a piece in the international chess game between the two superpowers.

The widening split with the United States also had important repercussions for Che's work as National Bank chairman. On the one hand, he had to try to prevent the flight of foreign currency from the island. On the other, he set about repatriating Cuban gold held in US banks, and searching for capable administrators for the businesses being brought into the state sector. Even so, he still found time to write and make important speeches on how he saw the revolution developing. By now he was thinking of how individuals needed to change in order to make a revolution that did not simply alter the ownership of the means of production, but had a direct and constant impact on daily lives. These thoughts were expressed on many occasions over the next five years, as he attempted to define what the "new" socialist man and woman should be. In August 1960 he put it this way:

> How does one reconcile individual effort with the needs of society? We again have to recall what each of our lives was like, what each of us did and thought... prior to the revolution. We have to do so with profound critical enthusiasm. And we will then conclude that almost everything we thought and felt in that past epoch should be filed away, and that a new type of human being should be created. And if each one of us is his own architect of that new human type, then creating that new type of human being—who will be the representative of the new Cuba—will be much easier.

On October 13, 1960 the Eisenhower administration declared a trade embargo on all goods to Cuba—apart from food and medicine. Castro fought back at once, nationalizing some 400 foreign banks, US-owned sugar plantations and factories. This was followed by what was known as urban reform, which granted title deeds to those living in foreign or privately-owned properties whose owners had left the island, and freezing rents. Foreign-owned mining companies were also nationalized. Still in position as the head of the industrialization program, Che had to try to administer all these new state-owned companies, and to find qualified people to manage them. All sorts of businesses—from the huge Bacardi rum company and de luxe Havana hotels to sugar mills and mines—were brought under state control, and no compensation was paid to their foreign owners (according to the US government, American businesses and individuals lost $1.8 billion in the process).

By now, the escalating tensions with the United States, and the 100,000 or more Cuban exiles who had fled across the Florida Straits, seemed to pose an immediate security challenge. A week after this wave of nationalizations, when asked on Cuban television if he thought the trade embargo was a prelude to an invasion, Che replied:

Like almost everybody else, I think they will come, and also like everybody else I don't think they'll be able to get out again. So what will the final result be? It will consolidate the revolution.

Before this prediction could be tested, however, Che set off again on another tour of the Soviet Union, China and several Eastern Bloc countries. He was successful in obtaining guarantees that Cuba's surplus sugar production (no longer being bought by the United States) would be taken up. He was also invited onto the podium in Moscow's Red Square to celebrate the "October revolution" alongside Premier Nikita Khrushchev, an honor usually reserved only for heads of state. This was probably the closest Che ever came to identifying with the Russian revolution as interpreted by the generation of leaders trying to move their country forward after years of rule by Josef Stalin: it would not be long before he became increasingly critical of their interpretation of socialist values, while they came to see him as a someone who might rock the boat in their cautious plans for the advancement of communism around the world.

One other person Che met during this visit who was to play an important role in the future was a German-Argentine woman called Tamara Bunke. She interpreted for him in East Germany, and soon afterwards came to Cuba, where she would later become intimately involved in his attempts to spread revolution to the rest of Latin America, including Bolivia.

It was soon after Che's return to Cuba that the military threat from the United States became real. On January 3, 1961 Washington broke off diplomatic relations with Cuba, to be followed by many other Caribbean and Latin American countries (with the notable exception of Mexico). Three months later, early on April 17, 1961, the long-anticipated invasion attempt by anti-Castro exiles, with the air and sea support of the United States, finally took place.

As soon as the Cuban government realized the invasion was imminent, Che was put in charge of the defense of the Pinar del

Río region, the most westerly on the island and thought to be the likeliest entry point for the invaders, as it was closest to the United States. Although in the end the attacks here proved to be a diversionary tactic, Che told the popular militia under his command:

> We don't know if this attack is the prelude to the announced invasion of five thousand gusanos ["worms," the pejorative term used by the Castro regime for those Cubans who had "turned" and gone to live in the United States]... But on the bodies of our fallen comrades, on the rubble of our bombed factories, with ever more determination we proclaim: *patria o muerte!* [fatherland or death!]

For many years afterwards, these words were to become the battle-cry of the Cuban revolution whenever it had to face any threat to its existence.

In the end, the attack did not come in Che's sector, but on the south side of the island at Playa Girón (The Bay of Pigs). It was Fidel Castro who masterminded the defense, and he was so successful that within three days the would-be invaders had been completely crushed. More than 100 of them were killed and almost 1,200 taken prisoner. (The prisoners subsequently became bartering chips between the two countries. After negotiations for their release stalled several times, they were finally despatched back to the United States late in 1962 in return for more than 60 million dollars worth of medical goods.) After the failure of the invasion attempt, many Cuban exiles blamed the new US president, John F. Kennedy, for his lukewarm support for their action. In the following year, however, he was to impinge on Cuba's destiny in an even more dramatic fashion.

The abortive invasion attempt accelerated the consolidation of power by Fidel Castro. On May 1, 1961 he made what was to become known as the Declaration of Havana, when he openly stated for the first time that the Cuban revolution was socialist in nature. At the same time, the July 26 Movement merged with the Revolutionary Directorate and Popular

Che and his trademark cigar

Socialist Party to create the Integrated Revolutionary Organizations (ORI), which were to be the vanguard of the continuing revolutionary process. Soon afterwards, the ORI became the Partido Unido de la Revolución Socialista de Cuba (PURSC), which in turn by 1965 had become the Communist Party of Cuba. In his speeches immediately after the Bay of Pigs victory, Fidel seemed as eager as Che for the example of the Cuban revolution to be taken up in other countries: "It is not for revolutionaries to sit in the doorways of their houses waiting for the corpse of imperialism to pass by," he declared.

Throughout the rest of 1961 Che Guevara was hard at work in government. By now, he had left the National Bank as he had been named Minister of Industry. In this post he was trying to cope with the many more businesses that had been nationalized as a result of the confrontation with Washington. He brought the same qualities to his ministerial post as he had shown in his days fighting in the sierra or in the months immediately after the revolutionary victory: complete immersion in the task at hand, disregard for himself, and an absolute determination to succeed. As Fidel Castro himself said years later:

> What a job he did—excellent! What discipline, what devotion, how studious he was, how self-sacrificing, how exemplary, how austere! Any job you gave him, he'd throw himself into, body and soul.

It was now that Che launched the idea of voluntary work, to be done by party and government officials at the weekend in order to keep them in touch with the reality of the ordinary working people of the new Cuba. He launched himself into this with all the enthusiasm he showed for every other task he took on, working twelve hours in the cane fields or on building sites after he had spent the other six days working up to seventeen hours daily in the ministry. Che was convinced that the only way to create a revolutionary consciousness was by example, and he took it upon himself to treat himself even more harshly than anyone else. He was never a person to deal in theory without immediately seeking to put it into practice.

The voluntary work had become necessary in order to meet the goals of social improvement the revolutionary government had set itself. But at the ministry, the difficulties of transforming a dependent, capitalist system into one run on socialist ideas were becoming increasingly plain. Production in the industrial sector was falling, at a time when the success of the revolution was leading to higher expectations. The problem of spare parts and replacements for machinery made in the US soon became pressing, while the heavy goods bought in the Soviet bloc were proving to be less technologically advanced and reliable than Che had at first thought. The question of wages and wage differentials also quickly raised its head: should people be paid more if they took on more responsible jobs, or should everyone be paid less, in order to create more employment and encourage egalitarianism? Che's speeches and writings from this period show that he was already considering this kind of dilemma, which eventually came to be part of his theory of the "new man" in socialist society.

While at home he was grappling with problems of how to make the revolution work on a day-to-day basis, outside Cuba Che was still seen as the romantic guerrilla leader. This was obvious when in August 1961 he went to the smart resort city of Punta del Este in Uruguay, for a conference of the Organization of American States (a regional organization of all the countries in the hemisphere regardless of their political tendencies, from which Cuba was suspended the following year). Che immediately became the star of the show, and was frequently mobbed by sympathetic Uruguayans. At the conference itself, he harangued his audience for more than two hours, calling for all the countries of the region to be able to choose their own political and economic orientation, independently of the United States and its ideological preferences. He also attacked the "Alliance for Progress" proposals that the Americans had brought to the table. This was President Kennedy's plan to offer support for moderate land reforms in Latin America and other social democratic measures designed to forestall any further revolutionary movements in the Caribbean or South America.

While in Punta del Este, Che had two significant meetings. The first of these was with President Kennedy's young envoy, Richard Goodwin. The two men conversed for up to an hour, with Che suggesting that Cuba was willing to talk to the Kennedy administration "without preconditions." But it is Goodwin's description of his first impressions of Che which is perhaps most revealing of him at this period:

> Che was wearing green fatigues, and his usual overgrown and scraggly beard. Behind the beard his features are quite soft, almost feminine, and his manner is intense. He has a good sense of humor, and there was considerable joking back and forth during the meeting. He seemed very ill at ease when we began to talk, but soon became relaxed and spoke freely. Although he left no doubt of his personal and intense devotion to communism, his conversation was free of propaganda and bombast. He spoke calmly, in a straightforward manner, and with the appearance of detachment and objectivity.

The next day, Che flew secretly to Buenos Aires to meet President Arturo Frondizi. This was the first time he had set foot in his homeland in eight years. Frondizi was a radical who led a government denied legitimacy because of the Argentine armed forces' refusal to allow the Peronists to participate in political life. He was interested in Guevara as a person as well as in his capacity as an emissary from the Castro government. Their meeting over lunch changed nothing in Argentina's strained relationship with Cuba, although it is said to have been one of the factors behind the military coup which led to Frondizi's overthrow a few months later.

By the time this coup took place early in 1962, Fidel Castro's attempts to enter into some kind of dialogue with the Kennedy administration were a thing of the past. In Cuba, the strains of the transition to a centrally-planned socialist economy were being felt ever more strongly. Despite Che's efforts to plan the newly state-run industries, production had continued to decline in many areas. The agricultural cooperatives which had replaced the big agro-concerns were also failing to reach the hoped-for goal of self-sufficiency in food. In March 1962, the Castro government found itself forced to introduce rationing of staple foodstuffs and other basic items (and rationing of many items has continued ever since).

But a far worse crisis was looming, one that brought the threat not only of the overthrow of the revolutionary government but the real possibility of a nuclear war that could engulf the entire planet. Ever since the attempted invasion at Playa Girón, the Cuban leadership had been concerned that the United States might make another, more determined, attempt to take over the island. As Fidel Castro took Cuba more closely into the Soviet Union's sphere of influence, the idea grew—and Che seems to have been among those who supported it—that in order to secure the island from any attack of this sort, they should establish a treaty with the USSR by which an invasion of Cuba would be seen as a hostile attack on the Soviet Union itself.

Meanwhile, in Moscow Premier Nikita Khrushchev was determined to resist American military pressure on the Soviet Union. The United States had recently installed long-range ballistic missiles in Turkey, which he saw as a direct threat to Russia. In response, Khrushchev and his politburo colleagues seem to have come up with the idea that the USSR should build up its arsenal in Cuba in order to present the United States with a similar kind of challenge on its own doorstep. Among the long list of military hardware Khrushchev wanted to offer Castro were two dozen medium-range and sixteen other ballistic missile launchers, which could be armed with nuclear warheads. The Soviet premier also offered to send more than 40,000 troops to operate all this weaponry and to act as a further deterrent.

By the end of July 1962, Castro had agreed to Khrushchev's proposal. He sent Che to Moscow to get the Soviet leader's signature on the final deal. Khrushchev in fact never did sign, arguing that there was time enough for such formalities once

Che the orator addresses a mass rally

everything was in place. Che also tried to extract answers from him as to what the USSR would do if the Americans discovered the secret agreement, but apparently received no satisfactory answer on this score either.

In the event, the Americans did quickly learn that the USSR was installing a missile system in Cuba. In October 1962 a US reconnaissance U-2 plane took photographs of what was clearly a missile base in construction in the western part of the island. After a three-way exchange of accusations, denials and threats, it seemed as though the world was on the brink of a nuclear war. Further Russian ships loaded with missiles were sailing towards the island, and President Kennedy issued his ultimatum that if they tried to get past a US naval blockade, they would be fired upon. For several days there was a standoff between Kennedy and Khrushchev, with neither of them willing to back down. In Cuba, the entire population was mobilized. As during the earlier invasion attempt, Che was despatched to Pinar del Río in the west. He set up his command headquarters in a network of local caves, apparently trusting that they could serve as a nuclear bunker if the looming war actually broke out.

In the end, nuclear disaster was averted. Kennedy and Khrushchev came to an agreement by which the USSR would remove its missiles from Cuba and install only "defensive" military equipment there. For its part, the US government promised to withdraw its ballistic missiles aimed at the Soviet Union from Turkey, and further agreed that it would make no attempt to invade Cuba.

Yet if the whole world breathed a sigh of relief, Castro, Che and the rest of the revolutionary leadership on the island were furious. They felt that Khrushchev had done the deal over their heads, without even consulting them. Che angrily told anyone who would listen that if the Cubans had been in charge of the nuclear missiles, he personally would have had no compunction about firing them if the US had made any move to attack.

Although the danger passed, the experience of being used as a pawn in a superpower game seems to have triggered a re-appraisal by Che of Cuba's relationship with the Soviet Union. Although he had initially been enthusiastic about help from the Soviet bloc countries in order to speed up Cuba's industrialization, he now felt that the island was simply exchanging one form of imperialism for another. He was also increasingly critical of Soviet society, which he thought had not advanced along the path of creating a different kind of "man," the socialist committed to following the old Marxism dictum "from each according to his abilities to each according to his needs," because it still offered financial incentives to workers and maintained a money-based economy. He was also impatient with the idea, promoted by the Communist Party in

Moscow, that conditions were not ripe for revolution in Latin America, and that there should therefore be a policy of "peaceful coexistence" towards the United States.

In September 1963 Che published a second version of his earlier work on the guerrilla experience, entitled: *Guerrilla Warfare—A Method*. Here he emphasised yet again his belief that a determined group of individuals banding together for a common cause could "jump-start" a revolution without having to wait for the "objective conditions" to exist. This armed vanguard would be "at the head of the working class in the struggle for power, [and would] know how to guide it towards seizure of that power, even leading it through short cuts."

This view was, and still remains, hard for traditional Marxists to accept. In a critique of the Argentine revolutionary, *Che Guevara and the Cuban Revolution*, for example, the veteran socialist Mike Gonzalez argues that:

> While he uses the term "working class," Che emphasizes over and over again in his essay that the guerrilla army must be located in the countryside, and recruit above all among the peasantry, because it is they who have suffered the most brutal exploitation. But suffering, of course, does not create revolutionaries. On the contrary, without collective organization and the confidence that comes from the experience of struggle, and without the power to strike at the very heart of capitalism—the machinery of production—suffering can produce despair and a sense of impotence.

Che had no such doubts. One of the conclusions to *Guerrilla Warfare—A Method* declares that violence is the only way to expose the oppressive heart of the regimes found in many Latin American countries:

> The dictatorship tries to function without resorting to force. Thus we must try to oblige the dictatorship to resort to violence, thereby unmasking its true nature as the dictatorship of the reactionary social classes.

This determination to confront the forces in power by military means as the first stage in the revolutionary takeover of power was to have disastrous consequences in the following decades when applied by insurgent groups in countries such as El Salvador and Guatemala.

In addition to his critique of the Soviet position on revolution, Che was caught up in fierce debates about the economic bases for carrying the revolutionary changes forward in Cuban society itself. These arguments were aired most notably in the pages of a new journal, *Nuestra Industria* (Our Industry), launched in June 1963. Che argued for centralized planning so that the state could have a proper overview of the whole economy, and help bring about the proper development of all sectors, rather than reinforcing difference and backwardness. He was also still keen to downplay the role of money, or "value," in the transition towards socialism. He argued that moral incentives were far more important, since "I'm not interested in an economic transformation unless it's accompanied by a socialist morality," he wrote.

What Che meant by this "socialist morality" was to be more fully defined in his 1965 essay *Socialismo y el hombre en Cuba* (Socialism and Man in Cuba), but for now it was the leaders of the INRA, the agrarian reform institute, who put forward a different economic model. They insisted that material incentives should not be eliminated, as they had proved to be the most effective way of boosting production. They also argued for a more decentralized economic model, preferring to allow individual businesses to manage their own affairs, and only taking any surplus generated for use by the state.

Meanwhile, the Guevara family continued to grow. On June 14, 1963 (Che's thirty-fifth birthday) he had his third child with Aleida, a girl they called Celia after his mother. The naming was particularly poignant because the birth coincided with Che's mother serving a three-month jail sentence in the women's prison in Buenos Aires. She had been arrested at the airport in Argentina after returning from spending several weeks with Che in Cuba. The military government in power at the time did not want any political agitation, and she was arrested for being a suspected Cuban agent. From this time on, as the regimes in Argentina became increasingly concerned with the "fight against communism" and so increasingly suspicious of the figure and influence of her son, Celia Guevara suffered many threats and acts of persecution before her early death in 1965, an event which affected Che deeply.

The revolutionary leader was always very close to his mother, and also seems to have enjoyed his life with Aleida and his Cuban children. A fourth child, another boy whom they called, almost inevitably, Ernesto, was born to the couple on February 24, 1965. Yet this picture of Che as a happy family man has been questioned by at least one of his biographers. Jorge Castañeda, the Mexican writer and diplomat, claims that Che fathered at least one child outside the marriage. He maintains that on March 19, 1964 Omar Pérez (supposedly named after the legendary Persian poet Omar Khayyam) was born to Lilia Pérez and Che. Che never officially acknowledged this child, nor parentage of any of the several other children he is rumored to have had.

The year 1964 was the year that decided Che's future. Fidel, his brother Raúl and the other revolutionary leaders were taking the island ever more closely into the Soviet sphere of influence. At the start of the year Fidel went to Moscow, where he was received as an important ally and friend. More importantly, he signed a six-year deal by which the Soviet Union agreed to buy most of the Cuban sugar crop at above world market prices. This agreement not only tied the Cuban economy more closely than ever before to the Soviet Union, but it also meant a renewed emphasis on a single agricultural crop as the mainstay of the Cuban economy. Most of Che's efforts as Minister of Industry had been precisely in the opposite direction, attempting to move Cuba away from over-dependency on sugar and agriculture. In July 1963, for example, he had told an audience in Algeria:

The single-product structure of our economy has not yet been overcome after four years of revolution. But the conditions are there for what in time might become an economy solidly based upon Cuban raw materials, with a diversified production and technical levels that will allow it to compete in world markets.

By early 1964, therefore, Che was increasingly isolated within government. No-one else was as adamant as him that to survive Cuba had to try to export its revolution to other countries, first and foremost in Latin America, but almost as importantly in other parts of the world. Fidel and the others were more concerned to establish the political stability that would allow Cuba to recover economically and socially, and help spread the revolutionary example on this basis. But the economic policies they pursued in order to achieve this goal were also anathema to Che. He was convinced that the only way to create a truly revolutionary society was by changing individual consciousness, and that the only way to do this was to change the system of values within society, removing all idea of material gain in favor of moral incentives. The market was to be replaced by the school, with all of Cuba's inhabitants learning how to transform themselves into "new" men and women no longer motivated by money but by socialist principles.

While increasingly diverging from Khrushchev and the other leaders in the Soviet Union, Che continued to explore the possibilities of communist and anti-imperialist governments and liberation movements elsewhere. By mid-1964 he was definitely looking for a way to become directly involved in another form of struggle. The Uruguayan writer Eduardo Galeano who interviewed him at the time, observed of him:

Che was not a desk man: he was a creator of revolutions, and it was apparent; he was not, or was in spite of himself, an administrator. Somehow, that tension of a caged lion that his apparent calm betrayed had to explode. He needed the sierra.

That urge seemed to be leading him inevitably towards Africa. In July 1963 he had visited Algeria, which had won its independence the year before after a long and vicious war against its colonial master, France. There is no doubt that Che saw Algeria as going through a process similar to Cuba, with the dominant imperial power just across the water, and continuing to exercise a huge and distorting pressure on Algerian attempts to create a new political, economic and social identity. He established a warm relationship with the new Algerian president, Ahmed Ben Bella. As well as discussing the revolutionary processes in their own countries, the two men are known to have talked of the prospects of revolution spreading elsewhere in Africa. It was probably during these talks that Che first began to consider the Central African state of Congo as a possible arena for further guerrilla action.

The end of 1964 saw Che making a number of decisive trips. They began in November with his second visit as a guest of the Soviet leadership at their October revolution celebrations. By now, Khrushchev had been replaced by Leonid Brezhnev, whose main aim was to reinforce loyalty to Moscow among Communist Parties around the world, especially in view of the widening split between the Soviet Union and China. Che, for his part, undoubtedly found himself closer to Beijing in his political sympathies, and the Moscow visit was the start of his practical moves to withdraw from the government in Cuba in order to pursue his own ideals elsewhere.

The next few months found him traveling the globe, delivering speeches against American imperialism, producing criticisms of the Soviet communist model and establishing contacts with "liberation fighters" in Africa. In December 1964 he paid his second and last visit to the United States, to address the General Assembly of the United Nations. He used his speech to reiterate Cuba's support for the liberation struggles going on throughout the Third World, as well as attacking imperialism for its support of the regimes in Southern Africa. He particularly incensed Washington by drawing direct parallels between anticolonial and anti-apartheid struggles and the fight for racial equality then at its height in the US. He further ruffled feathers when he met with representatives from Malcolm X's radical Nation of Islam movement.

From New York Che flew directly to Paris, the start of a tour of almost three months that first took him to China and North Korea, where he declared himself impressed by what he saw as "revolutionary spirit" enabling the country to rebuild from the devastation of the war that had split the Korean peninsula a decade earlier. After this, he visited many African countries, sounding out their leaders on the advisability of Cuba becoming involved in the rebel struggle in Congo and elsewhere. During his visit to Egypt, he is said to have been warned by President Gamal Abdel Nasser that he should avoid swooping into the Congo conflict "like Tarzan, a white man among blacks, leading and protecting them." To his cost, Che ignored the warning, and used the rest of his stay on the continent to drum up support for his initiative, and to plan its launch from the sympathetic haven of Zanzibar, which had recently won independence and was keen to offer help to revolutionary movements in other African countries.

Che's very last speech in public came in Algiers on February 24, 1965, to the Second Economic Seminar on Afro-Asian Solidarity. There he delivered a typically uncompromising message:

> There are no frontiers in this struggle to the death. We cannot remain indifferent in the face of what occurs in any part of the world. A victory for any country against imperialism is our victory, just as any country's defeat is our defeat.

He further went on to declare that the Soviet Union's reluctance to support liberation movements around the world was tantamount to betrayal. Even by Che's standards, this was an extremely outspoken declaration, and the Soviets are known to have been furious. When Che finally returned to Cuba on March 15, 1965, not only Fidel and Raúl Castro were there to meet him at the airport, but also President Osvaldo Dorticós

*Che addresses the General Assembly of the United Nations,
December 11, 1964*

and Carlos Rafael Rodríguez, the man who as head of INRA had questioned Che's economic policies. It is still unclear whether the four were there to show their support for him, or whether they were trying to smooth things over with Moscow by offering a display of official disapproval. What is known is that Fidel and Che had a discussion in private lasting many hours, and from that moment on, the Argentine revolutionary simply disappeared from public life.

His years in Cuba would soon be at an end, but in March 1965, before he left, he wrote one of his most famous texts: *El socialismo y el hombre nuevo en Cuba* (translated as *Man and Socialism in Cuba*). Significantly, this first appeared not in Cuba, but in the magazine *Marcha*, a left-wing magazine published down at the other end of the continent in Uruguay. In the essay he returns to the question of the individual under socialism. He repeats several times his fundamental belief:

> Man under socialism, despite his apparent standardization, is more complete; despite the lack of perfect machinery for it, his opportunities for expressing himself and making himself felt in the social organism are infinitely greater.

Once again, Che's revolutionary humanism is apparent throughout the essay. It is only under socialism that the individual can leave behind the alienation brought about under the capitalist system, where his labor is nothing more than a commodity, to be bought and sold without regard for him or her as a person. He sums up this belief in a neat syllogism:

> we socialists are freer because we are more fulfilled; we are more fulfilled because we are freer.

Addressing what he sees as the central problem of how the individual willingly gives up his self-centredness for the good of the community, he disagrees that in the revolutionary model the personal must disappear completely:

> it should be remembered that a Marxist is not a robot or a fanatic machine directed like a torpedo by a mechanism towards a determined object...

He admits that the individual consciousness exists beyond social relations, but insists that the individual

> has to achieve complete spiritual recreation through his own work, without the direct pressure of the social environment but bound to it by new habits.

The individual will come to feel it as a moral imperative that he or she devote his/her life to working for the good of the revolutionary community of which each one is an integral part, and will accept the surrender of the need to feel distance from the collective as a proof of self. This sacrifice of the selfish individual to the collective good, as Che argued on numerous occasions during the years after the triumph of the Cuban revolution, is something that demands hard work and sacrifice:

> one must have a large dose of humanity, a large dose of a sense of justice and truth in order to avoid dogmatic extremes, cold scholasticism, or an isolation from the masses. We must strive every day so that this love of living humanity is transformed into actual deeds, into acts that serve as examples, as a moving force.

What is unique in the essay, but is in many ways typical of Che's fusion of the political and the personal, is his insistence that at the root of the desire to bring revolutionary change to oppressive regimes is a feeling of love.

> The true revolutionary is guided by great feelings of love...It is impossible to think of a genuine revolutionary lacking this quality. Perhaps it is one of the great dramas of a leader that he or she must combine a passionate spirit with a cold intelligence and make painful decisions without flinching.

It is impossible not to see this as part of his bidding farewell to Cuba, as well as an attempt at self-justification in the eyes of history.

There is no doubt that Che was not a "desk man," and that he was anxious to be off to meet the next challenge. During his years as minister and bank chairman in Cuba Che had always supported guerrilla movements in other Latin American countries. Would-be guerrillas from Peru, Venezuela and Guatemala all received training and funds in Havana throughout the early 1960s. But closest to Che's heart was the idea that a revolution could be launched back in his native Argentina. Ever since 1962, he had been encouraging a group led by his old friend Jorge Masetti, with the idea of setting up a *foco*-style revolt in the jungle areas of north-west Argentina—one of the places he had visited on his motorcycle trip a decade earlier. For the moment though, it seemed that there was more opportunity to spread revolution in Africa than on his own continent. Che said hasty goodbyes to his family, promising Aleida that she could come and join him once he was well-established in his new country, and gave her his trusty watch: "the only gift he ever gave me," she ruefully remarked. He shaved off his beard and his flowing hair, donned a pair of thick-rimmed glasses and on April 1, 1965 left Cuba for an undisclosed destination. This time, however, his lucky star had deserted him.

5
HEART OF DARKNESS
(DEC. 1964–NOV. 1965)

When Che Guevara flew out of Cuba in April 1965, he left behind two farewell letters. One was to Fidel Castro (the consequences of the publication of this letter six months later are discussed below). The other was addressed to his parents in Buenos Aires. It opens with one of his most-often quoted phrases: "Once again I feel under my heels the ribs of Rocinante," he wrote, referring in mock-heroic tones to Don Quixote's famous broken-down nag. (His Cuban wife Aleida March said he had read *Don Quixote* at least half a dozen times, and was instrumental in its publication as the first mass-produced and cheap book launched by the revolutionary Cuban government in 1960.)

Although Che's critics have seized on this phrase to show he was nothing more than a revolutionary romantic, tilting at windmills as the man of La Mancha had done almost five hundred years earlier, Che's decision to leave Cuba in search of the next revolutionary challenge was born out of a deep political conviction. In his February 1965 speech in Algiers, he had insisted that,

> There can be socialism only if there is change in man's consciousness that will provoke a new fraternal attitude towards humanity on the individual level in the society which is building or has built socialism and also on a world level in relation to all the peoples who suffer imperialist oppression.

As ever, Che believed that his beliefs were worth nothing if they were not personally put into practice. He judged that thanks to his tireless work as a minister, he had helped place the Cuban revolution on a sound footing. Now he was determined to spread the lessons of that successful revolution.

As early as 1959 Che had hinted to Fidel Castro that his dearest wish was to bring this socialist revolution to his native country of Argentina. But his attempts to establish a forward base there in late 1963, with his Argentine colleague Jorge Masetti as leader, had been swiftly and ruthlessly crushed. Elsewhere in Latin America, Peruvian, Guatemalan and Venezuelan rebel groups had made little impact. In the Cari-bbean itself, Che had always been a fervent supporter of independence for Puerto Rico, in all but name a dependency of the United States. He had also followed closely the political unrest in the Dominican Republic after the assassination of the dictator Trujillo in 1961, but did not seem to consider that the conditions for a revolution could be found there or on any of the other islands.

Instead, he thought that Cuba's example could provide the spark for revolution in Africa. In the trips he made to that continent, where country after country was emerging from colonial rule at the start of the 1960s, he found willing listeners.

In Egypt, Nasser was keen to promote pan-African cooperation to oust the remaining colonial rulers. In Algeria, Ben Bella was also sympathetic to the idea of trying to unify anticolonial movements, as was Kwame Nkrumah in Ghana. Coming to Africa from the outside, Guevara underestimated the national and regional divergences between the newly-emerging nations. But in an interview with Josie Fanon, widow of the writer Franz Fanon, whose *The Wretched of the Earth* was one of the fundamental anti-colonialist texts, Che repeated that for him, Africa was one of the "most important fields of struggle against all forms of exploitation in the world—against imperialism, colonialism, and neo-colonialism." He stressed to her that the situation as he saw it offered real possibilities of success, as the entire continent seemed in ferment, but also recognized that it was the divisions among Africans—which he blamed on colonialism—that represented the greatest obstacle to revolution.

To kick-start that revolution, which Che hoped would spread through the whole African continent, he headed for what appeared to him to be a crucial anti-imperialist battle-ground: the central African republic of the Congo. This was where Joseph Conrad had situated his dark parable of the effects of European capitalism at the start of the twentieth century in *Heart of Darkness*. The Congo was rich in mineral and agricultural wealth, and Belgian colonial power, with direct rule from Brussels, lasted from 1908 until well after the Second World War. It was only in 1960, as many African states began to gain independence, that Belgium withdrew and allowed the Congolese to elect their own political leaders.

These first elections saw a pro-West politician, Joseph Kasavubu, voted in as president, while Prime Minister Patrice Lumumba was closer to the Soviet sphere of influence. It was not long before a power struggle broke out between the two men and their supporters. At the same time, the copper-rich province of Katanga declared its secession from the rest of the Congo. It backed up its claims to independence by bringing in Western-trained mercenaries to defend its territory. Lumumba called for 20,000 United Nations troops to come to the Congo to restore order and guarantee that the Katangan rebels and the mercenary forces did not take over the whole country. He also sought military aid from the Soviet Union, but this move backfired when it led almost immediately to a coup by the president, who had the backing of the regular Congolese army under General Mobutu. Soon afterwards, Lumumba was captured and murdered by the Katanga rebels, with the support of the CIA.

It was against this background of disorder and weak central rule that left-wing guerrilla groups formed the National Liberation Council. Their aim was to turn events to their advantage and bring about a revolution. By late 1964 they controlled a large area in the east of the Congo, and there seemed to be a real possibility that they might encircle the main cities and seize power—as had happened so successfully in Cuba only a few years earlier. Their cause was helped in the rest of Africa when Moises Tshombe wrested power from Kasavubu, and turned to the United States and the former colonial power Belgium to help bolster his regime. This left him isolated from the more progressive regimes in power in many of the other African countries, from Algeria and Egypt in the north, to Ghana and crucially Tanzania further south.

Che Guevara hoped to galvanize these "liberation fighters" by his presence and that of a hundred hand-picked black Cuban fighters on the ground in the Congo. His first impressions of the Congolese revolutionaries early in 1965 had not been very favorable. He suspected that they all preferred the lives of "professional revolutionaries," talking about revolution in congresses and meetings from Cairo to Dar-es-Salaam, rather than going into the mountains and becoming directly involved in the fighting.

The two main leaders he began to work with were Gaston Soumaliot, whose group had "liberated" a large area adjacent to Lake Tanganyika, which bordered on Tanzania, thus offering the rebels a safe refuge, and Laurent-Désiré Kabila, who was to play a part in the history of the Congo that went far beyond Che's experiences there. Kabila, as Che thought, was convinced that there was a role for international involvement in the Congo's liberation struggle, as the common enemy faced by the newly-emerging Third World countries was American imperialism.

After a roundabout trip via Moscow and Cairo, Che and the first group of his Cuban colleagues arrived in Dar es Salaam on April 19, 1965. From the first, their presence seems to have inspired suspicion as much as revolutionary fervor. Not knowing that Che was leading the group, the main figures of the National Liberation Council, apparently stuck in prolonged talks aimed at bringing about greater unity, did not come to greet the new arrivals in Tanzania. Despite their avowed enthusiasm for international support for their efforts, they were more concerned about carving out their share of power in a post-revolutionary Congo—which even Che thought would require at least five years of tough struggle.

Che did not stay for long in the safe haven of Tanzania. After a few days' rest, and despite the distinctly lukewarm welcome from those very leaders who were meant to be sponsoring these "international proletarian" attempts to gain control of the Congo, he embarked with his advance party of thirteen Cubans across the lake. The area to the west of Lake Tanganyika was under the control of the so-called People's Liberation Army. Che was at first impressed with the amount of weaponry they had, and by their apparent discipline. Initially, he seems to have hoped that the region with its high mountains and deep river valleys, flanked on one side by the friendly neighbors of Tanzania, could not only become a base for the Congolese guerrillas, but could also offer the opportunity of training left-wing forces from other African countries. One sign of such potential occurred when to their surprise, the Cubans found several thousand fighters from neighboring Rwanda in the area. They had joined the struggle in the hope that any revolution in the Congo could help hasten a return to their own country.

Che poses with Congolese member of guerrilla movement, 1965

When a further group of Cubans arrived in May 1965, Che decided to take direct control of the effort himself. He marched them and the African rebel groups away from the lakeside and up to a "base-camp" eight thousand feet up on nearby Mount

Luluabourg. After initial reconnoitring of the region, Che quickly came to some disagreeable conclusions. The atmosphere was very different from that of the Sierra Maestra. Most crucially, the local peasants had little faith in the "rebel" leaders. They were not well-known or popular figures, and few of the local inhabitants seemed to know what political ends they were fighting for. Che wrote of the Congolese leadership on the ground: "they spent days drinking, and then had huge meals without disguising what they were up to from the people around them. They used up petrol on pointless expeditions."

Although Kabila had not yet appeared in the mountains, he was keen to demonstrate that he was in charge. In June he ordered the rebel forces, Cubans and Rwandans included, to attack a government-held garrison in the town of Bendera, a strategic defense-point for an important hydro-electric plant. Che had his doubts about whether the rebel forces could succeed against a well-defended garrison, but he was considered too important a figure for Kabila and his lieutenants to allow him to take charge of the attack himself. In the end, the raid was a dismal failure: the Rwandan and Congolese spoke different languages, and the Cubans could not encourage either group to follow them into battle. Che wrote:

> Of the 160 men, 60 had deserted by the time of the engagement and many others did not manage to fire a shot. At the agreed hour, the Congolese opened fire on the barracks, nearly always shooting in the air because most of them kept their eyes shut and pressed the triggers of their automatic weapons until the ammunition ran out.

Worse than the rout itself was the fact that four Cubans were killed, and the discovery of identity papers on their bodies confirmed for the first time that Cubans were training the rebels. Although Che's presence in the Congo was still a secret, this internationalization of the conflict changed opinion in Africa and elsewhere around the world.

On the ground, some of the Cubans were already openly expressing their pessimism, and some even asked to return home. This seems to have taken Che by complete surprise. The "new men" whom he thought had been created by Cuban socialism were not quite all that he had hoped. The gloomy assessment in his diary shows his disillusion:

> at the first serious reverse, several comrades lost heart and decided to withdraw from a struggle they had sworn to come and die for, if necessary... what meaning does that phrase: "If necessary, unto death" have? In the answer to this lies the solution to the serious problems we face in the creation of our new men of tomorrow.

Less than two months into the Congo adventure, things were already looking grim. And at the end of May, Che received "the saddest news of the whole war"—the death of his mother from cancer at the age of 58 back in Buenos Aires. Celia had suffered political and social persecution because of her son's beliefs through most of the 1960s, and was even forced to move from one clinic to another in her final days, when the authorities in the first one she was taken to wanted nothing to do with "communists." The bond between son and mother was undoubtedly the strongest personal relationship Che ever had, and the fact that he wrote about it in his Congo diary gives some idea of how deeply her death affected him. As he noted in his diary, she had not even received the farewell letter he had written to her and his father back in March, which was only made public in October of that year, together with his goodbye letter to Fidel Castro.

After the rout at Bendera, Che insisted that the Congolese and Rwandans needed more training before they undertook any further offensive action. Again, he tried to repeat the lessons learned from the Sierra Maestra. He insisted that the troops undergo weapon and fitness training, and set up agricultural and productive facilities at the base camp. But he and his Cuban companions found it hard to make any political progress with the ordinary soldiers. There was no Fidel Castro to impose a sense of direction and purpose on the insurrection. As a doctor trained in Western medicine, Che found it hard to accept the supernatural beliefs that many of the men adhered to, especially when they argued that enemy bullets would not affect them if they had the *dawa* medicine that made them invulnerable.

Meanwhile, the Congolese rebel leaders were still mostly out of the country. Soumaliot even visited Cuba in August 1965, proclaiming that victory was near, yet there was no solid political plan for what the would-be "revolutionaries" hoped to achieve beyond taking power.

Eventually Kabila turned up in July, but stayed only the briefest time possible, and spent most of that trying to persuade Guevara to take his side in the event of a split in the "revolutionary" forces, and to promise not to help his rivals. Che's conclusion when the other man disappeared again after a few days is characteristic:

> We said goodbye, Kabila left, and activity in the base, which had begun to improve through his dynamic presence, grew slacker the very next day. Soldiers whose task it was to dig trenches said they would not work today because the leader had gone away; others who were building the hospital also abandoned their labors. Again everything began to acquire the easy, pastoral rhythm of our general staff—the rhythm of a village far from all the vicissitudes not only of war but even of life. Che's few moments of optimism came from his contacts with the ordinary peasants of the region, who, he said, were responsive to any human interest in them, thankful and cooperative.

By October the security of the rebel camp was under direct threat from well-organized mercenary forces supporting the Kasavubu government. These troops succeeded in occupying much of the territory previously held by the rebels, and as Che wrote in his diary: "we cannot liberate a country that does not want to fight." It was not long before their Mount Luluabourg position was overrun, forcing the rebels to retreat to the shores of Lake Tanganyika. It was at this time that Fidel Castro chose to make public the letter Che had written to him when he said goodbye to Cuba at the end of March. The letter itself reads like an eloquent political testament, and is worth quoting in full:

Fidel:

At this moment I remember many things: when I met you in Maria Antonia's house [in Mexico City], when you proposed I come along, all the tensions involved in the preparations. One day they came by and asked who should be notified in case of death, and the real possibility of it struck us all. Later we knew it was true, that in a revolution one wins or dies (if it is a real one). Many comrades fell along the way to victory.

Today everything has a less dramatic tone, because we are more mature, but the event repeats itself. I feel that I have fulfilled the part of my duty that tied me to the Cuban revolution in its territory, and I say farewell to you, to the comrades, to your people, who now are mine.

I formally resign my positions in the leadership of the party, my post as minister, my rank of commander, and my Cuban citizenship. Nothing legal binds me to Cuba. The only ties are of another nature—those that cannot be broken as can appointments to posts.

Reviewing my past life, I believe I have worked with sufficient integrity and dedication to consolidate the revolutionary triumph. My only serious failing was not having had more confidence in you from the first moments in the Sierra Maestra, and not having understood quickly enough your qualities as a leader and a revolutionary.

I have lived magnificent days, and at your side I felt the pride of belonging to our people in the brilliant yet sad days of the Caribbean [missile] crisis. Seldom has a statesman been as brilliant as you were in those days. I am also proud of having followed you without hesitation, of having identified with your way of thinking and of seeing and appraising dangers and principles.

Other nations of the world summon my modest efforts of assistance. I can do that which is denied you due to your responsibility as the head of Cuba, and the time has come for us to part.

You should know that I do so with a mixture of joy and sorrow. I leave here the purest of my hopes as a builder and the dearest of those I hold dear. And I leave a people who received me as a son. That wounds a part of my spirit. I carry to new battlefronts the faith that you taught me, the revolutionary spirit of my people, the feeling of fulfilling the most sacred of duties: to fight against imperialism wherever it may be. This is a source of strength, and more than heals the deepest of wounds.

I state once more that I free Cuba from all responsibility, except that which stems from its example. If my final hour finds me under other skies, my last thought will be of this people and especially of you. I am grateful for your teaching and your example, to which I shall try to be faithful up to the final consequences of my acts.

I have always been identified with the foreign policy of our revolution, and I continue to be. Wherever I am, I will feel the responsibility of being a Cuban revolutionary, and I shall behave as such. I am not sorry that I leave nothing material to my wife and children; I am happy it is that way. I ask nothing for them, as the state will provide them with enough to live on and receive an education.

I would have many things to say to you and to our people, but I feel they are unnecessary. Words cannot express what I would like them to, and there is no point in scribbling pages.

Castro has said that he had to make the contents of Che's letter public in Cuba early in October because the Central Commi-ttee of the newly-formed Communist Party was about to be announced, and there would have been widespread speculation as to why Guevara was not a member. But the effect of the letter in the Congo was catastrophic. The Cubans there saw Che's renunciation of Cuban citizenship and his withdrawal from all positions of responsibility in the Cuban government as little short of betrayal. Che himself once more felt a foreigner— and doubly so, since he was not only now regarded with suspicion by the Cubans, but also by the Congolese, who wondered who and what he really represented. In many ways, the publication of the letter was the last nail in the coffin of the Cuban involvement in the Congo.

Even so, Che was resolved to make a last stand and to fight to the finish if necessary. In the event, this military last-ditch battle was avoided at the cost of a political rout. On October 13, President Kasavubu got rid of Tshombe as prime minister, and promised to end the contracts of the white mercenaries fighting his cause. This and other compromises were enough to persuade other African heads of state to back the Kasavubu regime, and to end their support for attempts to overthrow him. Even President Nyerere of Tanzania, who had been the strongest champion of the Cuban effort to bring revolution to the region, now decided that the time was not ripe and withdrew his support. According to some versions, this change of heart was a result of direct pressure from Moscow, where Leonid Brezhnev was making strenuous attempts to displace China as the alternative to US influence in the region.

By the beginning of November, it was plain to Che that there was nothing left for the Cubans to do but cross Lake Tanganyika back to Tanzania. The Cuban incursion into the Congo had failed. He wrote in his diary:

> I was deeply pained at the thought of simply departing as we had come, leaving behind defenseless peasants and armed men whose poor battle sense left them effectively defenseless, defeated and with a feeling of betrayal.

The Cubans sailed out of the Congo on three small boats, and found refuge in Dar es Salaam. Most of the hundred or so Cuban survivors went straight back to Havana. Che stayed on in the Cuban embassy in the Tanzanian capital, trying as ever to make sense of the experience by writing about it. His diary of events begins starkly: "This is the story of a failure," he says at the outset, before going on to detail all the shortcomings of the Congolese rebels, his own Cuban combatants and the mistake he himself made. Perhaps because it was such a candid account of revolutionary failure, the book was kept under lock and key in Cuba for more than thirty years after Che had finished it. It was only published in Cuba in the late 1990s, while an English version appeared in the year 2000, called *The African Dream: Diaries of the Revolutionary War in the Congo.*

In his epilogue to this book, Che attempts to draw the conclusions from the six-month disaster. The first pages take the reader back to the days of the "motorcycle diaries." They are a description of the geography of the eastern Congo, written with an earnest simplicity that reminds us that it was only a little more than ten years since the young Ernesto Guevara had first left his middle-class, educated Argentine family to look for adventure in Latin America. He also adds some characteristic amateur anthropology, but soon comes to the crux of the matter: the peasants in this part of the Congo at least, he argues, simply had no problems of land ownership or feudalism. Instead, they cultivated where they wished, the fertile soil providing them with all their food needs. Although their farming techniques were primitive, they could lead independent lives. In circumstances such as these, Che reflects, what could any liberation army offer them? "Deep thought and research needs to be devoted to the problem of revolutionary tactics where the relations of production do not give rise to land hunger," he admits. In other words, the oppression of landlords inflicted on landless peasants was simply not there, and so there was not sufficient impulse for revolution, at least of the peasant revolt type he himself had stressed previously. This difficulty, he writes, makes it even more important to have inspirational leaders capable of convincing the local population that they could be better off with regime change and a move towards socialism.

With this in mind, Che could only express his deep disappointment at the rebel leaders he had come into contact with. For him, they bore most responsibility for the revolutionary failure, although he does not mince his words when talking about the ordinary rebel troops either:

> devoid of any coherent political education, they consequently lack revolutionary awareness or any forward-looking perspective beyond the traditional horizon of their tribal territory. Lazy and undisciplined, they are without any spirit

of combat or self-sacrifice... All of these traits make the soldier of the Congolese revolution the poorest example of a fighter I have ever come across.

Nor does Che spare the hundred or more Cubans who joined him in the revolutionary adventure. Too often, he complains, they considered themselves "superior beings" who could not relate to their fellow black Congolese—even refusing to share their food. And all too quickly, he admits, the Cubans allowed themselves to become demoralized and lose heart: it seemed to him they were not really committed to the international effort to spread revolution to a country not their own. Although the Cuban revolutionary leaders doubtless wanted to show solidarity for African nations as part of their recognition of the origins of a significant part of Cuban society, their culture and beliefs were not as close to those of the Congolese as they and Guevara himself had imagined.

In his diaries though, Che reserves some of the harshest words for himself:

> I tended to lose control in the way I reacted to things; for much of the time my attitude might have been described as complacent, but sometimes I displayed very bitter and wounding outbursts...

Above all, Che blamed himself for walking away from the fight and leaving the Congolese and Rwandan rebels as well as the local peasants to their fate. He does, however, try to end on a more optimistic note, almost willfully asserting that "a revolution is possible" in the Congo, and urging Castro and the Cuban leadership to continue to support the revolutionary efforts there and in other African countries.

Even while he was composing his *Diaries of the Revolutionary War in the Congo*, political events there only served to underline his failure. On November 25, 1965, General Mobutu deposed President Kasavubu. He proposed political reforms, which led to the disbanding of the rebel forces. Mobutu was to remain as dictator of the Congo for a further thirty years. When he was

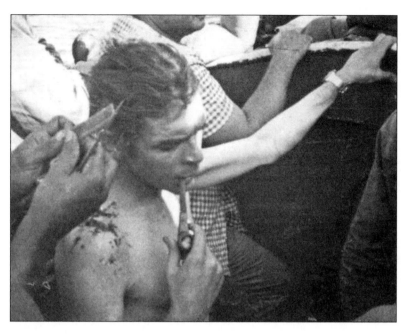

Che smokes a pipe while having his hair cut on Lake Tanganyika,
November 21, 1965

finally toppled in 1997, it was by someone Che Guevara would
have recognized: Laurent-Désiré Kabila. The socialist revolution
in the Congo was as far off as ever.

Although this was the end of Che Guevara's involvement
in Africa, Cuba itself would remain committed to the liberation
struggles there. Even before Che had been forced to pull out in
the eastern Congo, another group of some 200 Cuban fighters
was sent to Congo-Brazzaville, to start training the forces of
Agostinho Neto for guerrilla warfare in Angola, still controlled
by Portugal. Later, this effort was extended to Mozambique,
while through the 1970s and 1980s Cuban soldiers, as well as
military and other aid, were important in the fight against
minority white rule in Namibia and South Africa. Che
Guevara, however, did not live to see any of these successes.

6
A LONELY DEATH
(1966–1967)

During his time writing his military memoir in the Tanzanian capital of Dar es Salaam, Che saw few people apart from members of the Cuban intelligence services. In January 1966, his wife Aleida flew out to join him for several weeks. Despite the difficult situation, she described meeting and spending all this time on her own with him as her only real "honeymoon." He then spent several months in Prague, the capital of a Czechoslovakia, a country which in those days still appeared to be a loyal part of the Soviet Union. He told Aleida there that he did not want to go back to Cuba and return to a government position there. He felt that his letter to Fidel Castro, made public a few months earlier, had burned all his boats as far as Cuba was concerned. According to Castro in a 2005 interview, this was a question of personal pride: "Since he'd written a letter saying goodbye, and since he was so proud, it never occurred to him, after he'd said goodbye, to come back to Cuba." Guevara was also not someone who could accept defeat. The diary of the Congo debacle shows that he was even more determined now to find a suitable test case that would prove once and for all that his theory of peasant revolution was applicable to all those countries in the Third World that were struggling to combat imperialism.

This was his message to the Tricontinental (Africa, Asia and America) Conference held in Havana, which was published in Cuba in April 1967, after he had embarked on what was to prove his last, fatal foray into action. In his message he appealed to all those who wanted to see socialism triumph in the Third World. The enemy of everyone, he asserted, was US imperialism, which should be fought against everywhere: "Create two, three, many Vietnams," he urged his audience, recalling how the communist forces of North Vietnam were then engaged in a bitter struggle with South Vietnamese and US troops. He went on to describe how the revolutionary fighter should become "an effective, violent, seductive and cold killing machine," trying to engage the enemy wherever he had the opportunity, but taking the fight eventually inside the United States itself. The conclusion of his message reads like his own epitaph: Our every action is a battle cry against imperialism, and a battle hymn for the people's unity against the great enemy of mankind: the United States of America. Wherever death may surprise us, let it be welcome, provided that this, our battle cry, may have reached some receptive ear, and another hand may be extended to wield our weapons and other men be ready to intone the funeral dirge with the staccato singing of the machine-guns, and new battle cries of war and victory.

Although Castro accepted Che's refusal to return to a government position, he did succeed in persuading him to return to Cuba in order to organize another guerrilla expedition. Years earlier, when fighting in the Sierra Maestra in Cuba, Che had already written that Bolivia might be a good choice for such an expedition:

> I've got a plan. If some day I have to carry the revolution to the continent, I will set myself up in the jungle on the frontier between Bolivia and Brazil. I know the spot pretty well as I went there as a doctor. From there it is possible to put pressure on three or four countries and, by taking advantage of the frontiers and forests, you can work things so as never to be caught.

Just as in the Congo, the idea of the guerrilla *foco* spreading across borders and appealing directly to the oppressed, whatever the different countries in which they lived, was one of the most important factors in his decision to target Bolivia.

It seems to have been Castro, however, who finally persuaded Che that Bolivia was indeed the country in which his strategy of guerrilla warfare leading to a revolutionary takeover of power stood the greatest chance of success. There were several reasons for this optimism. On the one hand, a military government led by airforce commander René Barrientos had seized power in 1964, and unleashed fierce repression against the well-organized miners and other workers in the Central Obrera Boliviana (COB, the main Bolivian trade union grouping). In addition, the Bolivian Communist Party, although it supported Moscow's line of "peaceful coexistence" with the United States, could, Castro thought, be counted on for support for any guerrilla movement.

Che must also have considered that, if his Bolivian venture was successful, it would enable him to take the revolution across its borders to two countries close to his heart: Peru in the north and his native Argentina to the south. Henry Butterfield Ryan, who has written on Che's campaign in Bolivia, concludes that:

Castro did not simply send arms, money, and a few cadres, as in many other of his revolutionary attempts in Latin America… Instead, he sent Guevara with a band of some 16 stalwarts from Cuba's own revolution and ample resources to foment a major uprising.

In order to plan for the Bolivia guerrilla offensive, Che returned to Cuba in July 1966, in almost complete secrecy. In fact, when he arrived at Havana airport, a film crew from ICAIC, the Cuban national film institute, was filming a documentary there. When embarrassed intelligence officials spotted them, they stopped them filming and confiscated all their rolls of film, just in case the heavily-disguised figure of Guevara was spotted by any sharp-eyed spectator. Che went straight to a training camp in Pinar del Río, where only a few years earlier he had been in charge of resisting any invasion attempts by US-led forces. Now he embarked on a period of three months' intensive training with sixteen Cubans who had been handpicked by him and Fidel Castro to accompany him to Bolivia.

The German-Argentine agent Tamara Bunke or "Tania" had been acting as a liaison in the Bolivian capital La Paz for several months; in May an advance party of three men who had been with Che in the Congo also traveled there, to prepare the ground and try to guarantee support from the Bolivian Communist Party. Once again, while Che was training with the others in Pinar del Rio, Aleida visited him regularly. She occasionally brought their children along, although she did not reveal who they were visiting, saying only that he was an "old Uruguayan friend of your father's." Che also found time to discuss with another trusted friend, Armando Hart, the possibility of writing a philosophy textbook based on Marxist teachings ("but not like those Russian doorstops") for distribution to all Cuban schools.

Che himself continued to believe that even a small number of dedicated men could create enough insurrectionary momentum to build a revolution. He saw them as creating a spark that would attract the peasants who in Latin America still constituted the majority of the population, and who were forced to live—as he himself had seen in Guatemala and Central America a decade earlier—in feudal conditions where they owned no land and had few rights, often even being denied the right to vote or choose their political leaders at any level. As the rebellion grew, he argued, the elites in government would be forced to abandon any pretence that they were governing for the benefit of the people, and would show the "true" repressive nature of their regime, based on the abuse of power. A third stage would be reached, as had happened in Vietnam, when the threat of revolutionary takeover became so dangerous that the US "imperialist power," which backed all such regimes, would be forced to send its own troops to help quell the uprising. In turn, these foreign troops and the atrocities they committed would awaken the resentment of more and more people locally, who would inevitably turn to the guerrilla army and make it an irresistible force.

This was Che's blueprint for revolution, built on his experiences in Guatemala in 1954 and in Cuba leading up to the 1959 rebel victory. But despite the possibly favorable conditions mentioned above, Bolivia at that time does not seem to have been a good choice to implement his grand plan. After the 1952 nationalist revolution—which Che had witnessed—the country's tin mines, its main source of wealth, had been nationalized. The miners had helped form a strong, centralized trade union movement, the COB. They were in the political vanguard of resistance against the military government in the mid-1960s, and it was the Bolivian Communist Party (PCB) who had been most active in organizing them and helping them press their trade union, social and more overtly political demands.

Yet the Bolivian communists were split into two factions—those loyal to Moscow, and those who leaned more towards Peking. The former had more sway over the members, and in common with other Communist Parties throughout the Third World they accepted the Soviet argument that the time was not ripe for socialist revolution, as the "inherent contradictions of capitalism" had not yet made themselves manifest in a way that would make the overthrow of despotic regimes inevitable. Although in the first place Che was hoping to rally the peasants (whom he thought were landless, powerless and forced to live in conditions of abject poverty) behind his guerrilla movement, he also hoped to be able to call on support from the organized political opposition to the military regime—as had happened in Cuba's Sierra Maestra a decade earlier. In Cuba, this opposition had taken the form of Fidel Castro's own July 26 Movement, but in Bolivia the only option was the PCB. Soon after Che had embarked for Bolivia, Fidel Castro called its leader, Mario Monje, to Havana. He was informed clearly about what was going on, and persuaded to back Che's attempts to promote the armed struggle.

Guevara himself left Cuba towards the end of October 1966, under the false identity of Adolfo Mena González, a bespectacled middle-aged Uruguayan businessman. He met his contacts in La Paz on 3 November. Then he travelled by a circuitous route to the region where he had decided to create the *foco*, or guerrilla base. He crossed into the southeast of Bolivia from Brazil, and set up camp south of the city of Santa Cruz, in a place called Nancahuazú.

According to James Dunkerley, an academic expert on Bolivia, Che's choice could not have been worse:

> It would have been harder to find in all Bolivia an area less well-suited to the fighting of a guerrilla war, especially by the *foco* method... The area was one of broken hill chains, complex river systems and deep ravines; it offered good cover but was extraordinarily difficult to traverse and had no defensible perimeter... [It] was very sparsely populated and the peasants living there held land in adequate quantities, were highly parochial in outlook... and had never demonstrated any deep-seated discontent or proclivity for radical politics.

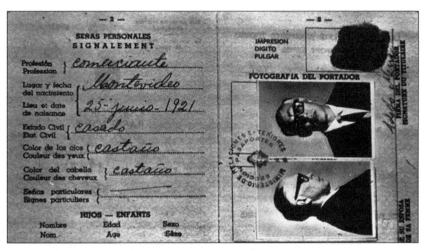

Che's fake passport photos, used to enter Bolivia

Che was by now well aware from his experiences in other Latin American countries and the Congo that peasants did not have a highly-developed political consciousness. But he always saw the neglect and isolation they suffered at the hands of almost all kinds of authority as a potentially explosive situation which could be quickly turned to advantage by a small but determined group of revolutionaries who on the one hand would make sure they were treated very differently, and on the other show them that positive change could be accomplished by taking up arms.

This at least was his fervent hope at the start of November 1966, when he set up camp with his group of a score of Cubans, Bolivians and Peruvians. At the same time, he as usual began a diary which detailed the daily events, explained (to Fidel?) what his reasons for taking certain decisions and actions had been, and served as a logbook for his own study in order to plan for the future. In his monthly summary at the end of November 1966, he wrote:

> Everything has gone fairly well: my arrival was uneventful. Half the men got here without trouble, though they were a bit late... The outlook appears to be good in this faraway region, where everything seems to indicate that we will be

able to stay for as long as we think necessary. The plans are: wait for the rest of the men, increase the number of Bolivians up to 20 at least, and start operating.

But he ended the summary on a more cautious note: "We still have to find out Monje's reaction."

That reaction was not long in coming, and it had disastrous consequences for the guerrilla group. Monje came out to the camp towards the end of December 1966, after visiting Fidel Castro in Cuba. Although the Cuban leader seemed convinced that Monje would throw his weight behind Che, the meeting between the communist leader and the guerrillas quickly reached an impasse. According to Guevara, Monje insisted he must be the leader of the guerrilla movement, with the Argentine revolutionary playing a subsidiary role. This was unacceptable to Che; he felt that the main reason for the failure of his Congo expedition had been the way in which he had placed himself at the orders of the local political leaders, who did not share either his agenda or his sense of urgency. He was also suspicious of Monje and the Bolivian Communist Party's commitment to the armed struggle. He therefore refused to budge over the question of who should lead the effort.

Monje left the camp on January 1, 1967, and from then on Che's fledgling National Liberation Army was on its own. Even Che's mentor Fidel Castro has recently expressed his reservations at Guevara's attitude towards the Bolivian communists and their leader:

> he found there were problems in the camp—a row between the leader of the Bolivian Communist Party, Mario Monje, who had some people there, and one of the leaders of an anti-Monje faction, a man named Moisés Guevara. Monje wanted to take over the command, and Che was very upright, very rigid... I think Che should have made a greater effort towards unity—that's my opinion.

But Fidel Castro was not there at the time to advise him— and radio links with Havana were only intermittent. In typical style, in January 1967 Che reacted to the disappointment of

Monje's withdrawal by organizing his tiny guerrilla army for a training operation. Early in February he set off with almost all of the men for a reconnoitring and toughening-up expedition in the dense scrub and jungle of the surrounding region. What had been intended as at most a two-week trip away from the base camp ended up taking a month and a half. During this time, the guerrilla group suffered hunger, disease, demoralization and the loss of two of its Bolivian members. Che's account of the death of one of these suggests his priorities at the time:

> The final result was the loss of several rucksacks, almost all the bullets, six guns, and one man: Carlos.

Alongside these entries, Che also carefully noted down the dates of all his family's birthdays, while other notes show he remained convinced that what he was doing in the depths of the Bolivian countryside was of international significance. The French intellectual Régis Debray, who had developed Che and Fidel's ideas on the revolutionary struggle in his own book *Revolution in the Revolution?* had come to visit the camp as an emissary from Castro, and on March 21, Che wrote:

> I must write letters to Jean-Paul Sartre and Bertrand Russell, so they can organize an international fund to raise money for the Bolivian liberation movement.

By this time, however, the immediate situation of the guerrilla group was a more pressing concern. Some of the local farmers near their camp at Nancahuazú had already told the military authorities of the suspicious presence of a group of men they thought were probably trafficking in cocaine or other contra-band across the Bolivian border. On March 23, the group of little more than forty fighters—sixteen Cubans, three Peruvians and twenty-nine—Bolivians—fought their first battle with Bolivian army forces. Che's men caught an army patrol of some sixty men by surprise, killing seven of them and capturing the rest. They also discovered the army's plans for advancing on and encircling the guerrilla band. Eventually,

Che let the soldiers go free, and gave permission for them to withdraw their dead over the next few days. As usual, he was harsher with his own men; he stripped some of their positions of command, and openly reprimanded several of the Bolivians for what he saw as their failings during the armed engagement. The combat did not serve to bring Cubans and Bolivians closer together, as he had hoped, but only exacerbated the tensions between them. Che was yet again learning the hard way that "international proletarianism" may be a fine concept in the abstract, but is much more difficult to achieve in reality.

There was now no way that they could keep their presence a secret from the Bolivian military. From the end of March, Che and his men were forced to keep on the move and to avoid as many as 1,500 troops trying to find and surround them. They had no time to make a proper camp, or to devote time to trying to win over the local inhabitants to their cause. As Che wrote repeatedly in his diary: "our peasant base is still undeveloped;" in fact, not a single new Bolivian recruit joined them. He decided the group would have to try to break out of the army's encirclement and try to begin operations again in a different region—as Fidel Castro had successfully done in Cuba a decade earlier. But as he moved out and allowed Régis Debray and the Argentine would-be revolutionary Ciro Bustos to leave, he made the mistake of splitting his group into three. Not only were the Frenchman and Bustos picked up almost immediately, but the rearguard group was overrun by a Bolivian army unit.

Nevertheless, at the end of April, Che wrote in his monthly roundup:

> To sum up: a month in which everything has evolved normally, considering the standard development of a guerrilla war. The morale of all the combatants is good because they have passed their first test as guerrilla fighters.

With the arrest of Debray and Bustos it soon became known around the world that the legendary Cuban guerrilla leader Che Guevara was somewhere in Bolivia. It was Régis Debray who also apparently confirmed to the Bolivian authorities that the

Cuban revolutionary was operating in the east of the country, which has led to him being accused of "betraying" Che and contributing to his death. Yet the Bolivian army was already pursuing the guerrilla group, and it was only a matter of time before they became completely sure who was leading it.

Debray, a former professor, soon realized that he was more of an armchair revolutionary than someone who could live and fight in the hostile mountains of eastern Bolivia. After a show trial lasting 53 days, shortly after Guevara's death the Frenchman was convicted and given a thirty-year jail sentence. He was released in 1970 after an international campaign to which even General Charles de Gaulle added his name, and went on to study the very different kind of revolution being attempted under President Allende in Chile.

Debray's revelation to the Bolivian military in April 1967 had resulted in at least one of Che's predictions coming true: in the United States the CIA decided it was time to send men of its own to monitor what was going on. But this was far from being the mass deployment of soldiers that had led President Lyndon B. Johnson into the quagmire of the Vietnamese war. Although US military personnel were involved in training the elite Rangers detachments of the Bolivian army, there was never any indication that Washington was sufficiently concerned about the threat Guevara posed in Bolivia to warrant the despatch of any sizeable number of combat troops. Instead, the Johnson administration authorized the sending of a detachment of "Green Berets" to advise the Bolivian army on counter-insurgency techniques, and recruited several Cuban CIA agents to head south. The best-known of these was Félix Rodríguez, a veteran of attempts to invade Cuba in the 1960s and, according to him at least, one of the men recruited to assassinate Fidel Castro on several occasions. Now his job was to positively identify Che's presence in Bolivia, as many in the CIA and the White House still thought he was already dead, killed either in the Congo or by Fidel Castro himself.

By the time Rodríguez arrived in Bolivia in August, the embattled guerrilla group was already close to collapse. After being cut off from his base camp, Che had no medicine to keep his asthma attacks at bay. From June 1967 on, he had to travel everywhere by mule. Most of his group's time and efforts were spent trying to find enough food to be able to keep going. The local peasants showed only terror whenever they appeared, there were still no new Bolivian recruits, and back in Cuba lack of contact with Che meant that it was decided not to send any more men or weapons.

Even so, Che and his dwindling band were still capable of carrying out small-scale successful operations. On July 7, for example, they took over the small town of Samaipata, surprising the military garrison there and seizing a considerable quantity of arms. The main reason for that attack, however, had been to try to find some fresh medicines for Che, and although the fighters ransacked the town pharmacy, they failed to find anything of use for their leader.

A month later, Che noted in his diary that of the six men who had come with him from Cuba

> two are dead, one has disappeared, two are wounded, and I have a case of asthma I am unable to control.

Worse was to follow. The second guerrilla column Che had put under the command of the Cuban "Joaquin" was ambushed by the army and wiped out, including "Tania." The only survivor from the group helped give the Bolivian authorities and their Cuban CIA advisors invaluable information about the size and position of Che's guerrilla force. On his side, when Che realized that the radio reports he was hearing about a guerrilla column being destroyed by the Bolivian army were probably true, he decided that the best thing to do was to try to escape the region they had been bogged down in for the past few months. He headed north, closer to the city of Santa Cruz, into higher mountains where he hoped to regroup and find some respite.

Towards the end of September, he and his men reached the little hamlet of La Higuera. By now, Che's diary reads as though it were written by someone who knows that the game is up—as with a chess player, Che's movements seem like those of someone facing the end by moving the pieces around in a desultory fashion, awaiting the inevitable checkmate. After losing more men at La Higuera, Che led the seventeen remaining guerrillas up a ravine to shelter in high woods. Despite the increasingly desperate situation, Che was remarkably upbeat, writing on October 7, 1967 that

> we have completed the eleventh month since the guerrilla began. It was a day without complications, even bucolic...

Soon afterwards, they met an old peasant woman, and realized that she would probably soon give their whereabouts away to the army. In response, Che set out marching again up a canyon until two in the morning of October 8. He still had time to write his diary entry for the day: the last he ever wrote. These final notes show how little idea he had of how close the end was:

> The seventeen of us went off under a small moon and the march was very tiresome and we left a lot of tracks in the canyon where we were; it has no houses nearby, but there are some potato fields irrigated by ditches from the same stream. At 0200 we halted to rest, because it was useless to go on advancing... the army issued a strange report about the presence of 250 men in Serrano to stop the passage of the encircled men, who are said to number 37; they locate our hiding-place between the Acero and Oro rivers. The news seems to be a red herring.

On October 8 a company of Bolivian Rangers was brought into the search for the guerrilla group. They surprised Che and his men by appearing higher up in a ravine, so that the only way out for the guerrillas was to try to force a way past them. This proved impossible, and on the same afternoon Che was taken prisoner after he was wounded in the leg and his rifle rendered useless by another bullet. He was taken to the tiny adobe schoolhouse in La Higuera, and kept there, bound and with his wound unattended, until the following day.

It was then that Colonel Zenteno Anaya and the Cuban CIA agent Rodríguez flew in from the nearby garrison town of Vallegrande to interrogate their prisoner. Anaya questioned him while Rodríguez was busy photographing the pages of his diary. Rodríguez, who later went on to help ship arms to the Contra forces opposed to the left-wing Sandinista government in Nicaragua and took part in the counter-insurgency efforts of the Salvadorean army against the guerrillas in that country, wrote in later years of his first sight of their prisoner:

> Che was lying on his side on the floor, his arms tied behind his back and his feet bound together. Near Che lay the corpses of two guerrillas... Che's leg wound was slightly, but visibly, oozing blood. He was a mess. Hair matted, clothes ragged and torn.

According to Rodríguez, at ten that morning he received radio instructions from the Bolivian high command that Guevara was to be shot. He claims that he told Colonel Zenteno that the CIA wanted to take Che up to their base in Panama for interrogation, and thought he was of much greater value alive than dead. Zenteno knew, however, that President Barrientos wanted the glory of being able to say that Che had been killed in combat in Bolivia, to show that he and his armed forces could succeed where so many others had failed.

Shortly after one o' clock on the afternoon of October 9, a Bolivian sergeant, Mario Terán, shot Che Guevara several times, deliberately aiming at his chest or lower to make it seem as though he had been killed while fighting. Che's last words to him are said to have been: "I know you've come to kill me. Shoot, coward, you are only going to kill a man."

Soon afterwards, Rodríguez strapped the body to the skids of an army helicopter, and flew with it back to Vallegrande. Che's body was then taken to the Nuestra Señora de Malta hospital, where the corpses of many of the other guerrillas killed in the last battle had been put on display. The photographs of the dead Che, eyes staring blindly, or with Bolivian army personnel staring avidly at the bullet wounds in his naked chest, were taken that same day.

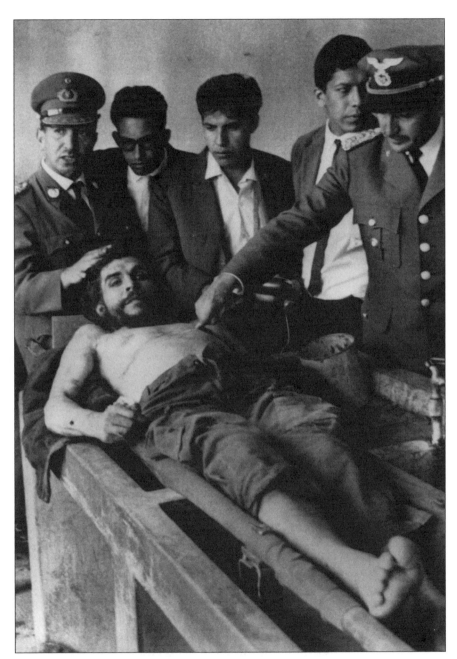

The body of Che Guevara in La Higuera, Bolivia

This was not the only outrage that his corpse suffered. In order to be able to convince the whole world that they had indeed killed the Argentine revolutionary, the Bolivian chief-of-staff General Ovando Candia ordered that his hands be chopped off. After this was done, he also ordered that Che be buried by the side of the runway of the Vallegrande airstrip.

Che's handless body stayed there for thirty years. His brother Roberto and others who enquired about its whereabouts were told that Che's corpse had been cremated. Members of the Bolivian military junta gave conflicting versions of the truth, but no attempt was made to inform the Cuban authorities, Che's wife Aleida March, or his family.

The mystery surrounding Che's burial site was in keeping with the aura surrounding many of his other exploits, and helped create the idea that he had somehow triumphed over his enemies even in death. Simultaneously, the "curse" on all those involved in his killing began to arise. The head of the military government General René Barrientos died in a helicopter accident in 1969. One of the Bolivian peasants who had given away the guerrillas' position to the authorities was shot by a new group of left-wing revolutionaries, also in 1969. Then, in 1971, the colonel who took Che's fingerprints was murdered in Germany. In 1976 General Joaquín Zenteno Anaya was shot in a Paris street by the previously unknown "Che Guevara International Brigade." Captain Gary Prado, who had been in charge during Che's final hours, was accidentally shot and left paralyzed from the waist down in 1981.

Bolivia continued to suffer from repeated military take-overs and short-lived, corrupt governments until the second half of the 1980s. It was not until 1997, when it was finally ruled by a stable and moderate civilian government, that the authorities permitted a team of Cuban forensic scientists to search for Che's remains.

In July 1997 his skeleton and those of six others were discovered. They were put into coffins and flown to Cuba.

Hearses carrying the remains of Che Guevara and those who died with him in Bolivia, leave the Revolution Square in Havana, October 14, 1997

In October 1997, after seven days of official mourning during which as many as a quarter of a million Cubans filed past his open coffin placed inside the monument to José Martí, the nineteenth-century independence hero, Che's and his companions' bodies were buried at the foot of a giant statue of the Argentine revolutionary in the provincial capital of Santa Clara, where he had fought a decisive battle almost forty years earlier. Insisting that the spirit of Che lived on, Fidel Castro stressed he was still "everywhere there is a just cause to defend." He concluded:

> Che is fighting and winning more battles than ever. Thank you, Che, for your history, your life, and your example. Thank you for coming to reinforce us in the difficult struggle in which we are engaged today to preserve the ideas for which you fought so hard.

7
THE LEGACY

When the news of Che's death was confirmed in Cuba, Fidel Castro declared a period of three days' national mourning. On October 18, 1967, he addressed a silent crowd of more than a million people in Havana's huge Revolution Square. He spoke of his personal anguish at losing a comrade and friend, and ended by looking to the future: "if we wish to express what we want our children to be, we must say from our hearts as ardent revolutionaries: we want them to be like Che!" Since then, each morning Cuban schoolchildren begin their day with the slogan: "Pioneers of Communism, we will be like Che!"

Portraits for sale: Che, Pope John Paul II and the Virgin Mary

The backdrop to Castro's speech was a huge, five-storey-high painting of Che's face, from the famous photograph taken by Korda six years earlier. This was the start of the transformation of Che the revolutionary fighter into Che the icon, a process that has continued unabated throughout the forty or more years since his death.

One of the first battles over Che Guevara's legacy arose over the diary he had kept during the Bolivia campaign. President Barrientos had the original, and immediately set about negotiating its sale to publishers in Europe and the United States. The highest offer was said to have been around $400,000, but the deal never took place. This was because photocopies of the original diary had been smuggled out of Bolivia soon after Che's death, and by July 1968 the Cuban government published a Spanish-language version, soon followed by editions in all the major European languages.

In Bolivia, the immediate impact of Che's death was the collapse of the incipient guerrilla movement. Only five of his group managed to escape the army's attacks; three Cubans eventually made it home after escaping over the Andes to Chile. The Bolivian Communist Party remained split throughout the 1960s into pro-Soviet and pro-Chinese wings, while those who supported the idea of a Guevara-style *foco* kept his name of the Ejercito de Liberación Nacional (National Liberation Army) and as late as 1973 were claiming a "vanguard" role for the coming revolution in Latin America.

The orthodox Marxist view of Che's Bolivia venture, however, is expressed by Mike Gonzalez:

> This was a terrible and costly failure born of Che's insistence that the will of the revolutionary can overcome objective conditions and substitute the individual for the movement of an entire class. That way lies martyrdom, not social revolution.

This appears also to have been the attitude of many of the top members of the government in Cuba. Despite Fidel's praise and genuine grief at the loss of such a companion, the general opinion among the Cuban leadership was that his Bolivia campaign had been badly planned and was too ambitious. By the end of 1967 and the start of 1968, Fidel Castro was becoming ever more closely aligned to Moscow, as Cuba depended to an increasing extent on the USSR and its allies buying most of its sugar harvest on advantageous terms. The process of industrialization that Che had championed in the early 1960s had already been largely abandoned in favor of importing goods at subsidised prices from the Eastern bloc.

Che's economic ideas, based on centralized planning and the distribution of any monetary surpluses throughout the system, with the stress on productivity rather than profitability and the use of voluntary labor as a means to change the concept of work, were largely left behind by the late 1960s and early 1970s, when more emphasis was placed on material incentives. Che's obvious hope that money itself could become unnecessary in a communist society was also quietly dropped, although there has been an almost constant tension ever since within Cuba between encouraging private initiative and the restriction of opportunities for individuals to make a profit from their skills and services, as well as the continued rejection of the idea that individuals can employ others to work for them.

Politically, a turning point for Cuba came with the so-called "Prague Spring" of 1968. When in August that year Soviet tanks moved into Czechoslovakia to put a stop to the timid efforts at liberalisation undertaken by the Czech communists under Prime Minister Alexander Dubcek, Fidel Castro explicitly backed the Soviet position. He soon followed this expression of support with a crackdown on dissent in Cuba.

Paradoxically perhaps, it was among youthful rebels in the developed capitalist world that the figure of Che Guevara took its strongest hold. Confronted with the Soviet invasion of Czechoslovakia on one side and the United States' war against the communist North Vietnamese on the other, many students and politically aware young people rejected both the super-power systems as morally bankrupt. This was the start of the process by which Che Guevara's legacy became important not so much for his specific ideas and proposals for making the socialist revolution, as for an "anti-authority" rebel status that was much closer to Mike Gonzalez's "martyr" or the poet Robert Lowell's "armed prophet."

The student protest movements that erupted across Europe and North America in the summer of 1968 adopted Che as a symbol of "imagination in power," the champion of a purifying violence that would sweep away all the old regimes and usher in a new, more democratic and freer system. Yet the capitalist system proved far more resilient than these young idealists hoped at the time. Although a few small groups in West Germany, Italy and France did continue to espouse the Guevarist idea that acts of violence were the most important and immediate way to expose the hypocrisy of the ruling classes—by demonstrating that their power was based on their monopoly on force—these were quite soon snuffed out by the efforts of state security forces.

In Latin America, Che's ideas on how to create a revolution had more impact. In his own country, Argentina, the late 1960s saw increasingly brutal military regimes attempting to stay in power by stifling all popular protest. The political response to this repression was complicated by the fact that the main opposition came from the Peronist movement, which had its own anti-imperialist rhetoric but was in no sense socialist in character. The situation became even more confused in 1973, when the Peronists returned to power. A small group of revolutionaries, the People's Revolutionary Army, (ERP) remained faithful to the Guevarist tradition and thought that they should oppose even a Peronist government, while more radical elements within Peronism tried to push the party towards revolution from the inside. Both attempts failed: the rural guerrillas were annihilated by the Argentine armed forces, who also toppled the Peronist government in 1976 and proceeded to eliminate all the radical Peronists, whether they were inspired by Guevara, Castro or anyone else.

It was perhaps in Central America that Che's ideas were followed most closely. In the early 1960s he had given encouragement as well as material and moral support to guerrilla movements in Guatemala, Honduras, El Salvador and Nicaragua. In Guatemala and Honduras, those revolutionaries who followed his ideas soon split from the Communist Party. They rejected the idea that the priority should be to develop the party until it was strong enough to take over power legally, in favor of an immediate revolutionary struggle. Similarly, in Nicaragua, the Frente Sandino de Liberación Nacional (FSLN), which was formed in 1959 to try to oust the Somoza dynasty, had separated from the official Communist Party as early as 1962. Its militants followed the revolutionary ideas of Fidel Castro and Che Guevara, seeking to fight the regime from the countryside and from exile in neighboring nations, until a mass popular awareness could help topple the regime.

The FSLN was the only revolutionary group to actually win power on the American mainland, when it forced Anastasio Somoza into exile in 1979 and set up a revolutionary government. But, as Che himself had prophesied early in the 1960s, Nicaragua and the other Central American countries proved to be too close, geographically speaking, to the imperialist power of the United States. No administration in Washington could possibly allow any left-wing revolution to take root there. Under President Ronald Reagan, the United States began backing another kind of armed rural guerrilla—the right-wing Contras—who destroyed any attempts by the Sandinista government to implement their revolutionary program. Although Fidel Castro warned them against it, the Sandinistas bowed to huge pressure from Washington, and held elections while there was virtual civil war in Nicaragua and they had still not been able to bring real material benefits to the majority of the population. In 1989 the Sandinistas lost the general elections, and the revolution was over.

In Nicaragua and El Salvador, the United States showed it had learned at least one lesson from Che Guevara. In his book on guerrilla warfare, he had insisted that the threat of a popular insurrection, as in Vietnam, would sooner or later lead to the involvement of significant numbers of US personnel. This foreign presence would help galvanize opposition both to them and to the government they were trying to shore up. But in the 1980s the Reagan administration in Washington poured in funds, military hardware, and training expertise to help bolster the regimes in El Salvador and Guatemala and oppose the Sandinistas, but was careful not to send in troops. Where these regimes had not been completely hijacked by one family as in Nicaragua, they succeeded, often in an extremely violent, illegal and anti-democratic way, in thwarting the threat.

By the end of the 1980s, the guerrilla threat on the Latin American mainland was largely a thing of the past. This coincided with the collapse of the Soviet Union and the vast process of change in Eastern Europe. With the rampant advance of global capitalism, and the sense of the "end of history" because there was only one superpower and one dominant economic system, the type of revolution advocated by Che Guevara began to seem more implausible than ever.

Although Fidel Castro, his brother Raúl and the other historic leaders of the guerrilla struggle in Cuba still held a firm grip on the reins of power on the island, by now the mid-1990s the revolution was struggling to survive without massive aid from the Soviet bloc. A "special period in time of peace" was instituted, and fresh sacrifices demanded from everybody, including the rationing of many goods and fuel. To survive, the government chose to develop not traditional industry but the tourist industry—a move that would doubtless have infuriated Guevara. Although he is still held up as a model for Cuban children, and his image is prominent alongside that of the other "heroes of the revolution," there is almost nothing left of his legacy in Cuba today.

Even so, in a 2005 interview, Fidel Castro himself repeated his belief that Che is a powerful symbol for today's world:

> He is one of the noblest, most extraordinary, most dis-interested men I've ever known, which would have no importance unless one believed that men like him exist by the million—millions and millions of them—within the masses. Men who distinguish themselves in a truly singular way couldn't do anything unless many millions like him had the embryo or the ability, the capacity, to acquire those qualities.

At the same time, Castro suggested how for many around the world the figure of Che Guevara has acquired a new relevance at the start of the twenty-first century. According to the Cuban leader who helped the Argentine revolutionary realize at least one of his dreams on a Caribbean island that became his home, "Che is an example. An indestructible moral force. His cause, his ideas, in this age of the fight against neo-liberal globalization, are triumphing."

While there is some wishful thinking in the suggestion that Che Guevara's cause is winning the battle against global capitalism, it is true that his image and influence remain surprisingly present in many areas of the world more than forty years after his death. The idea that Marxism can offer a solution to the increasing problems of poverty and injustice in the world has faded away almost completely, and yet the figure of Guevara continues to inspire young people in situations as different as Chiapas in southern Mexico where the Zapatista Army of National Liberation is seeking greater autonomy for indigenous peoples, to anti-capitalist protests in European and North American cities, where young people are looking for something beyond the consumerism and unbridled economic growth that threaten to destroy the planet.

Alongside the lasting importance of Che Guevara's image is a seemingly inexhaustible curiosity about the details of his life and revolutionary trajectory. In 2009, timed to coincide with the fiftieth anniversary of the Cuban Revolution, Hollywood director Steven's Soderbergh (*Sex, Lies and Videotape*) made not one but two high-budget films devoted to a close examination of Che's days in the Cuban Sierras and his agonizing death in Bolivia. Together with the 2004 film, *The Motorcycle Diaries*, these cinematic interpretations of the figure of Che offer new and apparently eager generations the chance to judge his life and actions in films that go a long way towards conveying the unique appeal felt by those who came into contact with him in real life.

Ultimately, Che Guevara is still seen by many as one of those rare individuals whose life was entirely consistent with his stated convictions: "the duty of a revolutionary is to make the revolution," he wrote, and he died at the age of thirty-nine following his beliefs.

SELECT BIBLIOGRAPHY

Works by Che Guevara in English translation:

Back on the Road: A Journey to Central America. Harvill Press, 2001.

Bolivian Diary. Pimlico, 2000.

Che Guevara Reader: Writings on Guerrilla Warfare, Politics and History. Ocean Press, 2003.

Critical Notes on Political Economy. Ocean Press, 2002.

Guerrilla Warfare. Ocean Press, 2003.

Our America and Theirs. Ocean Press, 2000.

Reminiscences of the Cuban Revolutionary War. Monthly Review Press, 1998.

Self-Portrait: Che Guevara. Ocean Press, 2005.

Socialism and Man in Cuba. Pathfinder Press, 1989.

The African Dream: the Diaries of the Revolutionary War in the Congo. Harvill Press, 2000.

The Great Debate on Political Economy. Ocean Press, 2006.

The Motorcycle Diaries: Notes on a Latin American Journey. Harper Perennial, 2004.

Books on Guevara, Cuba, Latin America, & the Caribbean:

Anderson, Jon Lee, *Che Guevara, A Revolutionary Life.* Grove Press, 1997.

Baker, Christopher P., *Cuba Classics: A Celebration of Vintage American Automobiles.* Interlink Publishing, 2004.

Butterfield Ryan, Henry, *The Fall of Che Guevara.* Oxford University Press, 1998.

Base, Ron (with photography by Donald Nausbaum), *Cuba: Portrait of an Island.* Interlink Publishing, 2005.

Castañeda, Jorge, *Compañero: the Life and Death of Che Guevara* (translated by Marina Castañeda). Bloomsbury, 1997.

Castro, Fidel (with Ignacio Ramonet), *My Life* (translated by Andrew Hurley). Allen Lane, 2007.

Debray, Régis: *La Guerrilla del Che.* Siglo Veintiuno editores, 1975.

Debray, Régis, *Revolution in the Revolution?* Penguin, 1968.

Dunkerley, James, *Rebellion in the Veins.* Verso, 1984.

Franqui, Carlos, *Diary of the Cuban Revolution.* Viking Press, 1980.

Gerassi, John: *Venceremos! The Speeches and Writings of Che Guevara.* Weidenfeld & Nicolson, 1969.

Gonzalez, Mike, *Che Guevara and the Cuban Revolution.* Bookmarks, 2004.

Gott, Richard: *Cuba, a New History.* Yale University Press, 2004.

Gott, Richard, *Rural Guerrillas in Latin America.* Penguin, 1973.

Guevara, Alfredo, *Tiempo de Fundación.* Iberautor Promociones Culturales, 2003.

Guevara Lynch, Ernesto, *Mi hijo el Che.* Plaza & Janes, 2000.

Hatchwell, Emily and Calder, Simon, *Cuba in Focus: A Guide to the People, Polotics, and Culture.* Interlink Publishing, 200

Hodges, Donald C., *The Legacy of Che Guevara: a Documentary Study.* Thames and Hudson, 1977.

Karol, K. S., *Guerrillas in Power: the Course of the Cuban Revolution.* Hill & Wang, 1970.

Lowy, Michael, *The Marxism of Che Guevara.* Monthly Review Press, 1973.

Martin, Lionel, *The Early Fidel.* Lyle Stuart Inc., 1978.

Quirk, Robert E., *Fidel Castro.* Norton, 1993.

Rodríguez, Félix I., and Weisman, John, *Shadow Warrior.* Simon & Schuster, 1989.

Salkey, Andrew, *Havana Journal.* Penguin, 1971.

Sculz, Tad, *Fidel: A Critical Portrait.* Hutchinson, 1986.

Stubbs, Jean, *Cuba: the Test of Time.* Latin America Bureau, 1989.

Taibo, Paco Ignacio II, *Ernesto Guevara también conocido como el Che.* Planeta Mexicana, 1996.

Thomas, Hugh, *Cuba, or the Pursuit of Freedom.* Penguin, 1971.

Trento, Angelo, *Castro and Cuba* (translated by Arthur Figliola) Interlink Publishing, 2000.

Ziff, Trisha (ed.), *Che Guevara: Revolutionary and Icon.* V&A Publications, 2006.

INDEX

Illustrations are indicated by **bold** *page numbers.*